Happy Birthday Mark.

Pete Jackson

BEAUJOLAIS

THE COMPLETE GUIDE

BEAUJOLAIS

THE COMPLETE GUIDE

GUY JACQUEMONT and PAUL MEREAUD

FOREWORD BY
PAUL BOCUSE

The English text in this book was translated
from the French by Anthony Roberts.

CONTENTS

INTRODUCTION

Nothing remains to be said, or written, about the Beaujolais. All the ground has been covered; in works ranging from slim academic volumes dealing with precise points to great tomes of composite history. For this reason, the literature of our region is exceedingly rich – in a sense, it is like a harvest of grapes, from which one may extract elements in small quantities, by the *tassée*, by the *pot*, or by the bottleful.

The Beaujolais has always had its lovers, poets, scholars, historians and painters. In our own time, the region abounds with famous men who do much to spread its fame and prestige; though a natural modesty on their part forbids us to mention their names. We are, however, at liberty to cite those who are no longer among the living, such as Jean Guillemet (with his Beaujolais Almanachs), Léon Foillard, Claude Geoffray and Jean Laborde. All these men are part of our history.

Why, then, have we compiled *Beaujolais, the Complete Guide*?

Perhaps because we feel that no

Guy JACQUEMONT

real letters patent for the wine of the Beaujolais yet exist.

More probably because the friendship between the two of us, born of a shared passion for the Beaujolais, has stimulated the wholehearted collaboration of many highly competent people in compiling this book.

For what makes *Beaujolais, the Complete Guide* special is the fact that it is not confined to the efforts of two co-authors. We have simply been the catalysts for a terrific chain reaction. Historians, writers, journalists, printers, wine-growers and wine-merchants have all contributed to this book, which is thus the work of a group of enthusiasts – not forgetting, of course, a remarkable photographer.

Beaujolais, the Complete Guide is like the wedding finery of a young bride. It is meant to glorify a *terroir* where men struggle and sweat to create wine which achieves the miraculous paradox of appearing both on bar counters and in the world's most famous restaurants. We have tried to make something of a firework display of this book and we hope that we have succeeded in shedding fresh light on our subject.

But who would imagine – especially in the month of November – that the Beaujolais has a past, that it possesses wines whose reputations are anything but *nouveau*?

People often talk about the Beaujolais' brilliant marketing methods, and cite with envy the unity of purpose shown by the entire region when each year's new wine goes out to be sold. Yet, during the nineteenth century, the Beaujolais won many awards, not only in France but at Turin, Brussels, London and New York, for its Morgons, its Chiroubles and its Fleuries. Many memorable dinners have been accompanied by these same wines, served on a basis of parity with the 'greats' of Bordeaux and Burgundy.

The fact is that the Beaujolais has been producing wines of prodigious quality for centuries, and the foremost names of French gastronomy have long been accustomed to serve them with their finest dishes. These are the *cru* wines that the growers and wine-merchants still seek to make better known.

Another aspect of Beaujolais creativity is shown in the labels on the region's wine bottles. We have made a collection of these labels, limiting ourselves to the creative areas within the region. Their diversity is astonishing: they range from the sober and informative to the portentous and parchment-like. Between these two extremes are a wide range of thematic labels, illustrating the countryside, the living environment, aspects of vineyard work, flora and fauna.

Throughout this book we have given pride of place to labels, and we would emphasize that we have done this not merely to display our collection, but as a way of illustrating the wines of the Beaujolais in their infinite variety.

Labels are full of life, after all. They represent the designer's art, the printer's craft and the grower's choice of decoration for his bottles. They acquire permanence of a sort because people collect them.

We have chosen labels which are still current, along with many that have passed into disuse. Maybe some growers now sell to different wine-merchants, or maybe certain clients have changed their suppliers . . . No matter, as long as the reader understands that time doesn't stand still in the Beaujolais, or anywhere else.

Paul MEREAUD

FOREWORD

Even when I was very small, I was used to hearing the word 'Beaujolais' used frequently, and I was lucky enough to identify what it meant at an early age. I must have been about six when I first went to the Beaujolais with my father to buy the celebrated barrels, *pièces*; my mother had 'put money aside' to pay for them. From September onwards, the main topic of conversation was the phenomenon of Beaujolais. Suddenly the weather assumed an overriding importance. My father kept a worried eye on the least cloud which might bring hail or storms to spoil the harvest.

It took me several years thereafter to sort out these early observations and impressions and understand the ways of Beaujolais, whom I assumed to be a very great man since we paid him visits, worried in case he got wet, and saved money for him!

So, one day in October we set off on our bikes to visit the Beaujolais, in a high state of excitement. After following the river Saône as far as Villefranche, we turned off towards Morgon through purple and copper-coloured vineyards dotted with houses built of golden stone. The first impression was favourable.

My father used to buy his wine at Morgon, from his friend Aufran, a former cellarman at the famous restaurant Léon de Lyon, whose creator, Léon Déan, at that time ran a wine business as well as an eating house. M Aufran and my father had worked together for eleven years, my father being the chef at Léon de Lyon. Daily consumption of Beaujolais in the restaurant ran at 220 litres or the entire contents of one barrel between the morning *casse-croûte*, lunch, dinner and individual glasses bought at the counter.

We arrived at our destination. After the usual polite greetings and enquiries after health and the weather, we got down to serious business. How was this year's Beaujolais coming along and – the crucial point – what was a barrel going to cost? Obviously, the price varied each year according to the harvest. The acquisition of these barrels represented a huge outlay for my father, because they had to be paid for on the nail. Some years, when business at the restaurant was poor, he found himself obliged to borrow from his brother (much against his will) to buy the wine.

Once this stage of the discussion had been completed, we went down into the sanctuary where Sieur Beaujolais was preparing himself for his arrival. A scent of wood, mingled with an odour of musty stone and humid earth floors, enveloped us; the atmosphere was cool and fragrant. Then the tasting began. One of the dried sausages hanging from the beam at the doorway was sacrificed for the occasion, along with some goat cheeses which were being dried and ripened in a wire meat-safe. The composite blend of smells delighted me and made me feel slightly giddy.

Finally, agreement was reached on the price and the day when the barrels would be collected. (A few years earlier, in my grandfather's time, barrels and tuns, *tonneaux*, would have been carried by a paddleboat named *Le Parisien*, which plied the Saône between Mâcon and Lyon, delivering its precious cargo as it went.) All these dealings led us to the bistro on the village square. This was a café-cum-tobacconist-cum-grocery-shop, where the official papers authorizing the transportation of the barrels were customarily filled in. Not infrequently, a local wine-grower would bring in a Beaujolais from the year of his birth, and the men would drink another toast, waxing lyrical about the 'gunflint' savour of Clos de Py Beaujolais (Clos de Py being the name of the place where the grapes were harvested).

Next came the storytelling: everyone vying to tell the best joke or real life story. Often these were the same year after year, but no one thought them any the worse and always laughed just as heartily.

The story that I remember best concerned the curate of Odenas, the village just beside Château de la Chaize. This memorable person, Georges Réthy by name, was later nominated to the parish of Collonges and presided at my first communion.

The curate of Odenas was no ordinary priest. During the 1914–18 war he had been a captain in a regiment of Chasseurs Alpins and he continued to wear vestiges of his military uniform while carrying out his duties as a pastor: puttees, beret and cape. He bore the insignia of the Legion of Honour in his buttonhole, and was as skilled in the use of the paint brush as he was at sprinkling holy water. Scenes of Beaujolais life were his favourite subjects for drawings and paintings. At the beginning of his time at Odenas, his relations with local men were uncertain, especially with those whose left-wing ideas were categorically 'red' (perhaps because of the wine?).

The curate's flock at that time consisted of women and children only. The worthy man of God would probably have adapted to this situation perfectly well, had it not been for an untoward incident.

One day, after some heavy rainstorms, the roof of the presbytery was found to be leaking. The curate decided to go to the mayor and village councillors for assistance. A

should get into the Beaujolais.) The thing was perfectly simple and the curate could do it himself. The curate listened, thanked them warmly, and went home.

The following Sunday, as the women and children gathered on the square in front of the church prior to High Mass, they met the curate walking in procession with four choirboys in the vanguard. He carried his bucket of holy water and his sprinkler, and he was wearing his full Corpus Christi regalia. The little group crossed the village, watched by the entire population with a mixture of slyness and bafflement. Slyest of all were the men sitting on the café terrace by the church; the ones who never set foot in the House of God, who didn't hold with religion, and thought the Sunday services only good for diverting the women.

The little group made its way up to the spring which fed the village water tower. Here, the curate blessed the water, and all five made their way back the way they had come. When he reached the square, the curate addressed the assembled crowd of people. 'I am aware', he said, 'that you never put water in your Beaujolais, but as of this evening you will all drink soup that is made with holy water!' From that day onwards, curate Réthy was adopted as a friend by the whole village, no matter what their beliefs.

After these excesses, my father and I returned to Collonges. The following day, we began preparing the cellar for the arrival of the barrels.

For me, going down into the cellar was always a thrilling business, I

suppose because of the darkness and the shadows. The smells of must and sulphur would catch my throat, especially when the barrels were being fumigated. This operation was very exciting: my father would direct the tiny blue flame held in his fingers into each of the barrels, one by one. At last, the day of delivery arrived. Each barrel had to be roped and lowered down the stairway into the cellar. My father, standing at the bottom, had to stop the barrel's descent. This I thought dangerous in the extreme, and I was terrified that he would be crushed by the weight.

From this time on, the Beaujolais required much care. We had to check regularly on each barrel, as the wood progressively absorbed the liquid. At the same time we had to ullage the casks and draw the wine off the lees that formed.

Then came the bottling. So he could recognize the *cru* Beaujolais from the rest, my father put different coloured rubber bands around the neck of each bottle.

Plenty of Beaujolais has flowed across the world since those days. When I took over from my father, I no longer had to do all the work I have just described. My good friend Georges Duboeuf still does it all for me, under the best possible

meeting was held at the town hall, beside the church, and the curate explained his problem. The mayor and councillors laughed and advised that he take a ladder, go up on the roof, and replace the broken tile – just as *they* did when leaks developed in their winery roofs. (It was, of course, out of the question that any water

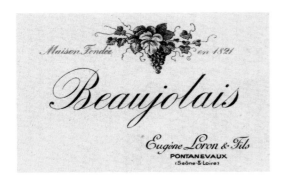

conditions; he possesses highly efficient machinery for every procedure, and as a result I receive the wine already bottled.

In the beginning, Beaujolais was a *petit vin*, known only to locals and to the people of Lyon. It was much favoured by men playing *boule*. I can still remember those sunny Sundays of my childhood, when my father would put the forty-six-centilitre jugs into buckets of cold water in the shade of the plane trees. Here the *boule* players would come to refresh themselves after a hard game, and be served by women in bright dresses.

The hour of glory for Beaujolais came on the day that a shrewd group of wine-growers brought it to Paris. It caught on immediately. Ever since then, the arrival of Beaujolais Nouveau has been celebrated like the birth of a baby; each year, the event grows in importance, as the reputation of the wine attains new pinnacles. Today it is known all over the world. I myself have contributed actively towards promoting Beaujolais in Japan and, more especially, in the United States. The agent who handles my distribution in the latter, an Englishman with a remarkable talent for public relations, had the excellent idea of organizing a carefully orchestrated annual twelve-day tour for me, throughout the principal states. At each stopover in a new city, a meal was prepared by us at the home of one of the foremost citizens. About a dozen people would be invited, including representatives of TV, press and radio. I would go out and do the shopping in person, accompanied by the lady of the house, and then we would do the cooking together. The meals were accompanied by Beaujolais (naturally) and the great *crus* of our region.

This formula produced more publicity than any five-hundred-seat gala could ever have done.

The following day, we travelled on to a different town; sometimes we went through as many as ten per tour. Like itinerant performers, each evening we mounted our show all over again.

In the same way, with my wine-merchants, I sounded out French-speaking African countries for several years, accompanied by our precious baggage of wines, *andouillettes*, sausages and local cheeses.

Everywhere we went, we laid on enormous elevenses, *Mâchons*, in the Lyonnais style, in the grounds of big hotels, serving the various foods and wines we had brought with us. Cool Beaujolais flowed by the gallon, to the evident delight of guests, hoteliers and nightclub-owners alike. The timing of the meals, at the end of the morning, was particularly appreciated, and the formula was highly successful in creating a new clientele.

Before us, Alexis Lichine, one of the main exporters of Beaujolais to the United States, had already made great progress by organizing trophies and competitions centred on Beaujolais wines. Closer to home, Jean-Baptiste Troisgros, serving Beaujolais cooled in ice-buckets, has made substantial contributions; and now every chef in the region is set on producing dishes that marry Beaujolais with local specialities like *coq au vin de Juliénas, oeufs pochés beaujolaise aux crôutons à l'ail, boeuf au Moulin-à-Vent, andouillettes au Beaujolais* and others.

Before herbicides began to be used on the vines, wild peaches, *pêches de vigne*, and blackcurrants, *cassis*, were abundant. A favourite wine-grower's

dessert was wild peaches sliced into a large glass, topped with a few blackcurrants and soaked in Beaujolais – delicious.

I am an unconditional lover of the Beaujolais, and I am now the lucky owner of a small vineyard in the region, at Létra. The wine-grower who looks after the harvest there, M Antonin Coquard, is president of the local cooperative winery; he has helped me to fill the gaps in my knowledge, by including me in every stage of the making of wine. This has made me feel closer to both vines and wine-growers, and I often go to Létra – whenever I can, in fact – to share the morning *casse-croûte* and exchange wisdom; for, in their way, these men of the land are great philosophers.

I remember a remark made by Joannes Papillon, during a trip to the United States organized by Georges Duboeuf and myself. We had invited along a group of wine-growers, and M Papillon was the doyen of the team. We were at the top of a New York skyscraper, on the ninety-ninth floor. It was about ten o'clock at night and we could see the city lights twinkling all around us. Suddenly Joannes Papillon burst out: 'But, the skies have fallen!' It was a perfect description, just as you would expect from one of those marvellous people, the wine-growers of the Beaujolais.

Today, I am deeply flattered to have been asked to preface this excellent book, which deals with the Beaujolais far better than I could ever do.

It was a shared passion for collecting wine-labels that originally brought together the two sponsors and organizers of *Beaujolais, the Complete Guide*, Doctor Paul Mereaud and Guy Jacquemont. The superb labels that adorn these pages are the fruit of many years' patient work, and they are admirably complemented by marvellous photographs taken by Pierre Cottin.

I offer my best wishes, along with my fullest admiration, to everyone who has collaborated on this book. The result is of a very high quality.

Et Vive le Beaujolais!

Paul Bocuse

The cloister of Salles

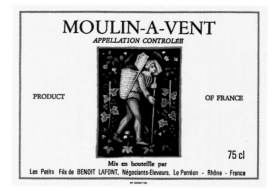

Jean-Jaques PIGNARD

There was once a shrub that could make men burst into song. Or rather, its fruit, when turned into a subtle beverage, had the power to warm their hearts and souls. It is said that the Lord gave grapes to Noah after the Flood, as a gesture of apology for having rained down so much water; and thus the vine and the juice thereof came into the world.

But when were vines first planted in the Beaujolais? Scholars still thirst to know. There is every reason to believe that the vine was established here as early as the Gallo-Roman era, before the Beaujolais existed as an independent entity. Mathieu Méras, a distinguished and erudite curator of the region's archives, states that the first document which explicitly mentions a vineyard in the Beaujolais dates from the year 956. The vineyard in question is that of Brulliacus, otherwise known as Brouilly; the mystical hill which, according to other less reliable sources, was shaped by the hand of Gargantua himself to guard the approaches to the vineyard.

Thus, when the lords of Beaujeu were campaigning beyond the Saône, they already had their Beaujolais to give them heart. In the same way, the bellringer at Rouen fortified himself with Beaujolais when he had to toll *la Rigaude*, the great bronze bell given to the cathedral by the Chanoine de la Rigaudière of Saint-Julien. The chiming of the bell was noticeably more joyous when the ringer had drunk *à tire la Rigaude*, as the phrase went.

The Benedictine monks of Cluny, who came to build a priory in the Salles valley, were also familiar with the cultivation of the vine. They liked it so much that they carved a bunch of grapes among the Romanesque stone capitals that still adorn their lovely cloister.

As to the treasure of the Templars,

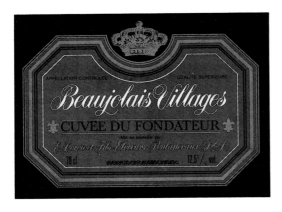

which is said to be buried in the Beaujolais district beneath the enigmatic towers of the Château d'Arginy, was it not simply the precious liquid brought forth by the autumn of each year, like Isis perpetually reborn in her cloak of pearly light?

THE BEAUJOLAIS UNDER THE BOURBONS

For over a hundred years, the king's close relatives held sway over the hills and valleys of the region without, for all that, attaching much importance to them. One of these Bourbons, Pierre, married Louis XI's daughter, Anne, maliciously described by her father as being 'of all the women in France, the least foolish', it being understood that there was nothing wise about her either. Anne de Beaujeu, as she is known to history, was regent of France during the minority of her brother Charles.

Anne bestowed the greater part of her patronage on the town of Villefranche, where she paid for the building of a clocktower for the collegiate church. In 1514, she designated Villefranche the new capital of the Beaujolais. Ten years later, her son-in-law the Constable de Bourbon betrayed François I and the Beaujolais district was annexed to the Crown, thereby losing its last vestiges of independence. Nobody much cared, for by now the hemp and grain trades had begun to enrich the local merchant families and bourgeois cloth manufacturers; the wine of the region, which travelled badly, was not yet a strong economic factor. At Villefranche, elegant Italianaté houses with turrets and balconies rose on either side of the main street. Indeed it was Italian architecture, as imported by the French kings following their various campaigns on

Habit de
Negociant beaujolais,

A Paris, Chez N de L'Armessin Rüe St Jacq.^s à la Pome d'or. Avec Priuil. du Roy.

17

Moulin-à-Vent

Appellation Moulin-à-Vent Contrôlée

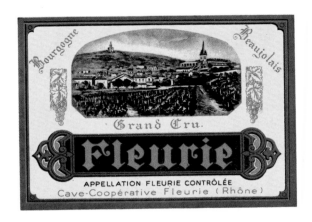

Bourgogne Beaujolais

Grand Cru.

Fleurie

APPELLATION FLEURIE CONTRÔLÉE

Cave-Coopérative Fleurie (Rhône)

CHIROUBLES

APPELLATION CONTROLEE

DOMAINE DU MOULIN

Mis en bouteille par E. LORON et Fils · Pontanevaux (France)   70 cl

PRODUCE OF FRANCE

Mont Brouilly (painting by Hugrel)

18

the other side of the Alps, which set the tone for this period of local Renaissance.

LOUIS XIV'S VISIT TO THE BEAUJOLAIS

Louis XIV came to the Beaujolais in 1658. At Villefranche, he stayed in the house of Mignot de Bussy. Louis was twenty years old at the time, but he would have had trouble passing muster as an army recruit at the *fête des conscrits*. Fortunately this had not yet been invented. Along with the Queen Mother, Cardinal Mazarin and the Grande Mademoiselle, he was making his way in leisurely style to Spain. There he was to marry the unfortunate Infanta, to whom he spent the rest of his life being unfaithful; dallying with the likes of Mme de Vallière and Mme de Montespan. Apart from that of François I, this was the only royal visit ever paid to the Beaujolais.

Perhaps it was Louis who, on recalling his brief stay in the area, in 1695 granted letters patent to the Académie Royale de Villefranche et du Beaujolais, only the fifth academy of its kind in France to be so honoured. At all events, at the dawn of the Enlightenment, the birth of this learned society (which 300 years later still shows no signs of losing its

La Félicité Parfaite.

vitality) was eloquent proof that the cultivation of the vine was in no way an obstacle to a cultivated mind. Anyway, was not Brossette, Boileau's eminent correspondent, a native of Théizé, a pretty village in the Pierres Dorées district?

THE RISE AND FALL OF MME ROLAND

Among the bourgeois who assiduously attended the Academy at the turn of the seventeenth century, there was one middle-aged gentleman who entranced his colleagues by the extent of his knowledge. It must be admitted that Roland de La Platière was hardly a newcomer. A native of the region, who held the post of *Inspecteur des Manufactures de Lyon* and whose career had also taken him to Amiens and Paris, he owned a house in Villefranche in which he spent the winter months and another at Theizé for the summer. A high official of the time, he had a young wife from Paris, Manon Philipon, the daughter of an enameller. Transplanted from the banks of the Seine to those of the Saône, Manon grew rapidly bored, caught as she was between her old fogey of a husband and an omnipresent mother-in-law. The girl was a romantic who idolized Rousseau, and her domestic situation guaranteed her a life of maximum stress which she sought to forget by maintaining a steady stream of correspondence with her friends in Paris.

Thus, Manon became the Beaujolais equivalent of Mme de Sévigné, despite her generally low opinion of the region. Villefranche and its 'sewer-like' streets offered scant inspiration to the letter-writer; moreover, she found the Caladois (citizens of Villefranche) boorish and ignorant of the arts of love. It is true that it was the fashion in eighteenth-century Paris to mingle those arts with adroit philosophical speculation.

Madame Roland preferred her summer residence at Theizé, with its picturesque festival and grape harvest. She participated in these events in the same way that Mme de Sévigné helped with the hay-making

Les Mangeurs de Raisins.

– which is to say, she confined herself to writing about them.

When the Revolution broke out in Paris, Mme Roland was on fire to contribute her portion to the march of history. Clearly, the future of France was not going to be decided at Villefranche-sur-Saône or at Theizé; so she went to Paris and opened a political and literary salon. Soon the wife of the official from the Beaujolais had become the muse of the Girondin revolutionary faction. Roland, who had accompanied his wife to the capital, found himself Minister of the Interior; but it was Manon who was the real power in the family, and she was soon immersed in the power struggle between the Girondins and Robespierre.

Sadly, she had picked the wrong side, and lost her head, as was the fashion of the times, at the guillotine. Did she really have time to utter the famous words which are attributed to her: *Liberté, que de crimes on commet en ton nom*? She probably did. It is hard to believe that a woman of letters worth her salt would consent to die without saying her piece.

At the time that Madame Roland was mounting the scaffold, the Beaujolais had been nothing more than a province of the realm for over 300 years. Now it was to become a mere district, *arrondissement*, within the department of the Rhône.

La Grange-Charton, the Domaine of the Hospices de Beaujeu

Scalding the vines

THE WINE-GROWERS

Anyone who imagines that the wine-growers, *vignerons*, of the Beaujolais spend their time sunk in melancholy does not know them. Beaujolais: these three syllables, which were once blazoned, like a challenge, on the banners of knights, would soon serve to ensure the lasting fame of countless wine-growers.

A tout venant, Beaujeu, 'I am ready to take on all-comers' was the war cry of the old seigneurs.* *A tout venant le Beaujolais* was now to be the response of the region's wine-growers.

The history of the Beaujolais under its old nobility ends with the sixteenth century; which also marked the beginning of the wine-growing Beaujolais as we know it. It was at this time, and more particularly in the centuries that followed, that grapes first became the predominant, then the exclusive, agricultural product of the area. Other crops were marginalized and eventually eliminated in an evolution which took 300 years to accomplish. The demand from Lyon and subsequently from Paris, when the opening of the Briare canal made it possible (though still difficult) to transport wine to the capital, was crucial in accomplishing the change. Until the sixteenth century, the vine stocks of the Beaujolais had been concentrated in the valleys around regional towns and abbeys; now they were to invade the

*A play on words: *jouer beau jeu* means: to play fair.

BENOIT RACLET.

hill slopes, with their better soils and exposures. Of course, at that time there were no *appellations controlées* (guaranteed vintages); but the various soil-zones of the locality, whose names are today synonymous with great vineyards, were beginning their slow metamorphosis. At the same time a special Beaujolais system of viticulture was evolving, a system which survives to this day and which gives the region its unique character: *vigneronnage*. This system is kin to the sharecropping, *metayage*, usually practised on wood and pasture land, though it has changed considerably over the years. There are no large

estates in the Beaujolais, as in Burgundy and Bordeaux; only small and medium-sized properties. The Château de La Chaize, which extended over the Odenas district at the height of the seventeenth century, consisted of hundreds, even thousands, of small landholdings, *voisinées*, upon which the loyal wine-grower and his debonair squire lived in relative harmony. Contracts were concluded at Martinmas; the harvest was shared out and farmhands were hired, at the fair at Villié . . . and when the wine-grower died, his son inherited his vines.

In the seventeenth century, another prominent character in Beaujolais life appeared on the scene. This was the wine-merchant, *négociant*, whose crucial importance has been demonstrated by the recent work of Professor Georges Durand. It was thanks to the wine-merchant that Beaujolais wine, which began as the 'filthy Gamay', *vilain Gamay*, so roundly abused by Philippe le Hardi, acquired its letters of nobility. On the eve of the Revolution, the Quais de Bercy in Paris, the old wine port and depot of the capital, overflowed with happy, motley crowds as the pot-bellied barges arrived at the dock with their cargoes of wine-filled bottles. The UIVB label (of the Beaujolais wine-growers' union) had not yet begun to decorate the taverns, but already the arrival of *Beaujolais Nouveau* was a matter for celebration. For the nobility of Beaujolais may simply be that of ordinary folk, who always loved it, even though the great

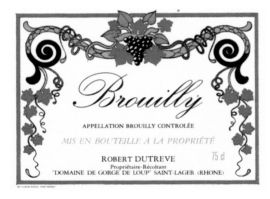

lords at court favoured more aristocratic wines.

It has a spark about it . . . and perhaps in 1789, when the new wine arrived at Bercy, just round the corner from the Bastille, it absorbed for all time the heady perfume of Revolution.

WORM AND CATERPILLAR

It was during the nineteenth century that the vineyards of the Beaujolais attained the dimensions we know today. At the same time, however, they had to cope with a succession of scourges which spread ruin and despair before they were overcome. First came the *ver coquin*, the grub of the bee moth, pyralis. Many a *Pater* and *Ave* were directed at the Holy Virgin of Montmerle, who was supposed to protect against this pest; but to no avail. The Virgin, who had once crushed the Serpent himself, might stamp her heel as much as she liked; but the wretched 'worm' always seemed to elude her and to continue to suck the marrow from the vines.

This went on until the July Monarchy, when Benoît Raclet, a Romanèche wine-grower, noticed that the only vine the worm had not damaged was right beneath the window from which his kitchenmaid threw out the hot dishwater. From here it was only a short step for Raclet to conclude that the eggs of pyralis could be destroyed by pouring hot water on each plant; which, with a *paysan*'s calm assurance, he proceeded to do. Thus Benoît Raclet saved the Beaujolais from the first great threat to its existence.

Forty years later, Victor Pulliat of Chiroubles emerged as a second saviour. This time the menace was even greater; phylloxera, appearing first in the Languedoc region, had gradually spread through all the vineyards of France. It reached the Beaujolais in the early 1880s; hill after hill, vine after vine, leaf after leaf, the disease-carrying caterpillar methodically went about its deadly work. When it had done, the region looked like a battlefield on the eve of a massive defeat. The wine-growers deserted their vines by the thousand to seek precarious employment in the workshops of Belleville and

Villefranche. Within ten years, the canton of Beaujeu had lost nearly half its population. The agricultural societies heard paper after paper proposing solutions, but the helpless oenologists could only stand by and watch as the ruin spread. Finally, after years of research and failure, several scientists (among them Victor Pulliat) arrived simultaneously at the long hoped-for solution: grafting local vines on to American rootstock. The vineyards were rebuilt too rapidly and on too large a scale for a national market which was in no shape to absorb a flood of new wine. The result was that the early years of the twentieth century were marred by over-production; wine prices plummeted. The wine-growers and their families, who had returned home from the cities, found themselves once more a prey to poverty.

But soon all Europe, gripped by war-fever, was to send its young men to the trenches of the Western Front. For the conscripts of the Beaujolais, the harvest of 1914 was a harvest of blood.

THE VIRGIN OF BROUILLY

Between the pyralis plague and the onset of phylloxera, another massive disaster struck the region's wine industry. At the start of the Second Empire, an epidemic of vine-mildew ravaged the country for several successive years. All efforts to control it were in vain. Finally, a group of growers decided that the Holy Virgin, if pressed, might be able to accomplish something, if only to banish the memory of her failure to conquer pyralis. After all, in the case of pyralis, there had been extenuating circumstances: a chapel had been built for our Lady at Montmerle on the other side of the Saône, in the *pays des ventres jaunes* (yellow-belly country), instead of among the *boyaux rouges* (red guts). These were the names by which the two rival communities on either side of the river were accustomed to call each other. The idea of building an oratory to the Virgin in the midst of the Beaujolais quickly gained favour. But where should it be sited? At Beaujeu, obviously, said some, on the site of the old feudal *château*. Others preferred Brouilly, in the very heart of the ravaged vineyards.

Brouilly finally carried the day and 1856 saw the raising of the oratory of Notre-Dame du Raisin on its hilltop. The mildew abruptly faded away. True believers were convinced that a miracle had taken place; but there was a small lobby which timidly maintained that the use of sulphur on the vines had perhaps been more effective than the prayers of the devout.

Whatever the truth may be, the Virgin has kept her vigil on her beacon for over a hundred years. Every year, on her birthday, a procession of wine-growers climbs the hillside to drink her health. For better or for worse, Notre-Dame de Brouilly is now a feature of the landscape. After all, as Father Pradel would say, she was 'the mother of a strange Messiah, who could tell His friends when they were assembled for a final meal together, "I am the true vine, and my Father is the husbandman".'

THE WINE OF VICTORY

1945 brought us the wine of victory.

It flowed from every press in every vineyard of the country; the presses swelled with the pride of this wine and with all the qualities that have made its name world famous.

Delicate, pungent, heady, silky, *satin en bouteille* – it is all of these and to perfection. It is a wine 'whose elements so harmonize and blossom on the palate, as to give the sensation of a peacock's spreading tail', to borrow the words of a gourmet archbishop of bygone times.

The brilliant summer of that glorious year blended and produced the quality of its wine. 1945 is a vintage which will be recorded in letters of gold among the great vintages of France.

Extract from *L'Almanach du Beaujolais*, 1946

" J'habite sur les coteaux du
Beaujolais qui font face à la
Dombes. J'ai pour horizon les Alpes
dont j'aperçois les cimes blanches
quand le ciel est clair. Je suis à
la lettre noyé dans des étendues
sans bornes de vignes qui donne-
-raient au pays un aspect mo-
-notone s'il n'était coupé par
des vallées ombragées et par des
ruisseaux qui descendent des mon-
-tagnes vers la Saône ".

Claude Bernard

Robert PINET

When I was a small boy, my parents gave me a marvellous book, richly illustrated by Uncle Hansi: *The History of Alsace*. One of the pictures, relating to the Revolution, showed the bridge at Kehl, built out of wood, with a sentry standing guard under a sign which said: '*Ici commence le pays de la Liberté*'. This picture affected me strongly, and I have always thought that we should raise signs around the borders of our own Beaujolais, bearing the words '*Ici commence le Beaujolais, pays de la douceur de vivre*'. The sentry would not be necessary.

The traveller who wishes to explore our region and savour its delights should not confine himself to the *autoroute* or the RN6 between Mâcon and Lyon. His first priority should be to leave the major roads well behind him.

BALANCE AND HARMONY

Just south of Romanèche-Thorins is an old boundary stone which has

marked the confines of the Beaujolais since well before the 1789 Revolution. Turn right opposite this stone and drive towards the mountains; before you have gone far you will be captivated by the pervasive calm of the surrounding landscape. The vines appear almost immediately, ascending the hills in serried ranks like advancing regiments. The road meanders somewhat drunkenly around them, in keeping with the area's exclusive dedication to wine, which is the fountainhead of its fame world-wide. For the very name of Beaujolais evokes the clear, fruity product of these vines, so appreciated and revered by connoisseurs.

Jean Guillermet, the native poet of the Beaujolais, described this region as a *Pays d'harmonie et d'équilibre*. The landscape is undulating, almost feminine, with gentle slopes and small pebbly streams. The broad expanse of

vines, which might otherwise have been monotonous, is studded with fine houses and clumps of trees. The whole scene is one of abundance and delight; it exudes what the French call *douceur de vivre*.

When I rhapsodize about the landscape of the Beaujolais, I am in good company. Edouard Herriot, for example, maintained that if there were such a thing as an earthly paradise, it was to be found here. Colette and Utrillo, to name two others, were deeply attached to the valley of the Saône. It is hard to resist these peaceful villages – yet they are often places of earthy realism; Belleville, for example, which used to be known as the Saint-Denis of the lords of Beaujeu. This little town is built by a mill-race diverted from the Ardières, a large stream (or small river) which flows from the mountains above Beaujeu. From time immemorial, this was used by washerwomen who, leaning over stones slanted into the water, laundered their fellow citizens' dirty clothes. In our time, of course, there are no more washerwomen, but the mill-race is still there, and the street that runs along it brings back memories of them. Their brazen character is vividly recalled by the name given to this place by the people of Belleville – *Rue du Canon Braqué* (Street of the Primed Canon). Nevertheless, as you wander further across the Beaujolais, you will find its people hospitable; they smile as you pass and are quick to offer the traditional cupful, *tassée*.

AT THE TOP OF THE FÛT D'AVENAS

In the northern part of the Beaujolais, the vineyards straddle the highest mountains in the range. By the time you reach here, you will have crossed the Fleurie district, leaving four famous villages on your right: Saint-Amour, a name which seems almost predestined to be famous; Chénas, with its old *château* (now the headquarters of the local wine-grower's cooperative) overlooking Moulin-à-Vent; Jullié, clinging to its hillside; and Juliénas, which has been so well depicted in the sketches of Henri Monnier, another Beaujolais native.

From here, press on as far as the Fût d'Avenas, a pass – or rather a belvedere – at an altitude of nearly 900 metres. From this spot the entire region is visible. At your feet are stretches of vines, beyond these the Saône, and finally the broad plateau of La Bresse and La Dombes. In clear weather, Mont Blanc is well within sight, with l'Aiguille Verte and Le Cervin to its left. Finally, much further to the north, there is the outline of a snowy pyramid: the Jungfrau.

Just behind the pass, stop at the Avenas Church and admire its Romanesque altarpiece, which has been a persistent headache to many an archaeologist; no one has yet put a

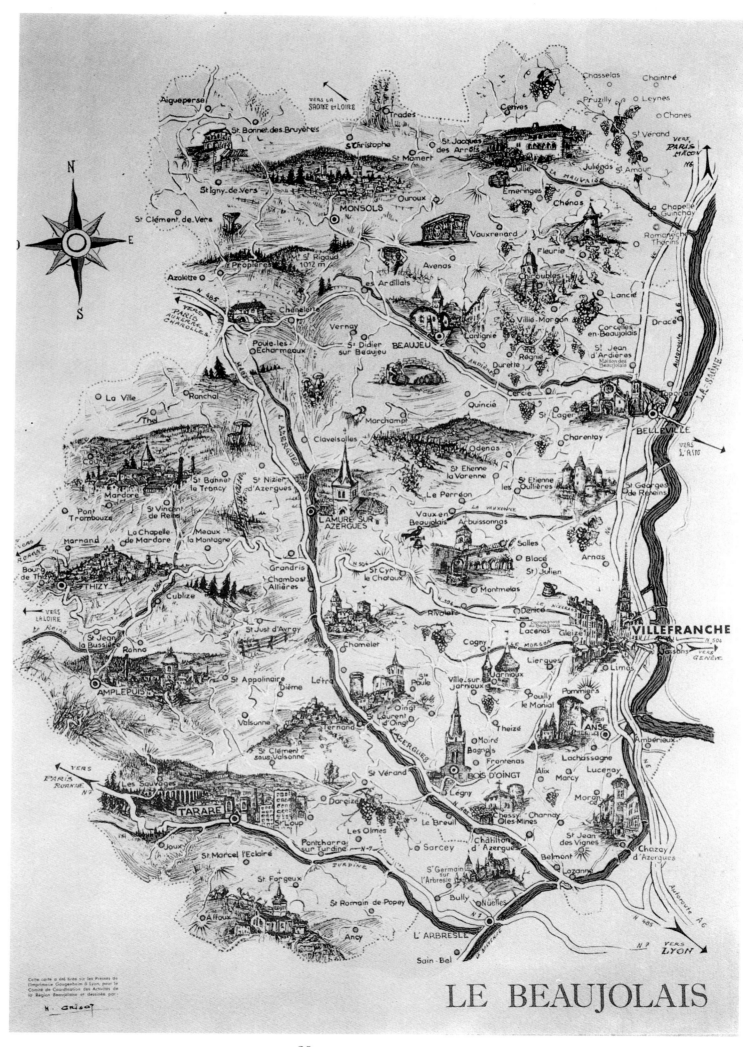

LE BEAUJOLAIS

MON BEAUJOLAIS

O Beaujolais, val ou colline,
J'aime à pétrir de mes deux mains
Ta rouge terre dont l'échine
Craque au soleil et boit du vin.

Chaque pays a son mystère.
Le mien rit, en biberonnant.
Le chais où mûrit la lumière
Ouvre sa porte à tout venant.

Mieux qu'un Palais ou qu'un Empire
J'adore un toit sur mon coteau;
Mes ancêtres l'ont vu reluire
Et mon fils apprend ce qu'il vaut.

Au pays des moulins d'en face,
La belle appelle son meunier;
Chez nous le grain pousse à l'audace..
Et l'amour veille en nos cuviers.

Fût-il seigneur en sa Bourgogne,
Nul n'est jaloux de son voisin.
A chacun selon sa besogne,
Heureux qui peut mouiller son pain !

Nous le mouillons tous à la ronde,
Tant et si bien que nos tonneaux,
Plutôt que de courir le monde
Se débondent sur nos tréteaux.

S'il me fallait partir en guerre,
Dans la musette du « mâchon »,
De ce Morgon qu'a fait mon père,
J'emporterais un bon canon.

Moulin-à-Vent, Chénas, Fleurie...
Et du Chiroubles... et du Brouilly.
J'en voudrais aussi, ma patrie,
Pour mieux t'épouser, loin d'ici.

Mourir ici ou là, qu'importe
A la raison d'un buveur d'eau !
. . . .
Il nous faut le sillon qui porte
La promesse d'un vin nouveau.

P. THOMANN
EXTRAIT DE L'*ALMANACH DU BEAUJOLAIS*, 1952

date to it. A charter at Saint-Vincent de Mâcon would seem to show that a hospice run by nuns once stood here, till it was pillaged in the eighth century by a band of Arabs, who raped and murdered the inmates; but this is not certain. And which King Louis was it who built the church and its altar? Nobody knows. It is, however, reliably reported that Julius Caesar pursued the fleeing Helvetic tribes across this pass, after he had defeated them for the first time on the banks of the Saône. They fell back to Bibracta, the Gaulish citadel at Mont Beuvray near Autun, where they were caught and annihilated.

GANELON'S BARREL

From here, drive back in the direction of Beaujeu. The road meanders, steeply at first, through the woods; then emerges to overlook the valley of the Ardières. If you come here at the end of May, or at the beginning of June, you will be astounded by the beauty of the yellow gorse which covers these hills. Beaujeu is at the bottom of the valley.

The entire landscape is dominated by the cone-like Tourvéon. Popular legend relates that Ganelon, the betrayer of Roland, had his castle on this site. A few remains may still be

The belltower at Jarnioux

GRAND VIN DU BEAUJOLAIS

CHÉNAS

APPELLATION CHÉNAS CONTRÔLÉE

CHATEAU DES JEAN LORON

DOMAINE DESVIGNES, LA CHAPELLE-DE-GUINCHAY (S.-&-L.) 71

12,5 % vol 70 cl

Château de Raousset

CHIROUBLES

Appellation Chiroubles Contrôlée

Sélectionné et mis en bouteilles par
P. FERRAUD - 69220 BELLEVILLE

DOMAINE DU PRIEURÉ

RENÉ PIN, PROPRIÉTAIRE

MOULIN-A-VENT

APPELLATION MOULIN-A-VENT CONTRÔLÉE

75 cl

MIS EN BOUTEILLE PAR R. SARRAU, SAINT-JEAN-D'ARDIÈRES, RHONE, FRANCE

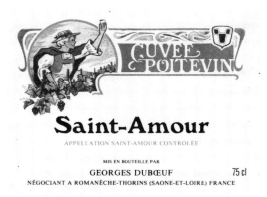

found on the mountaintop, but even as early as the mid-sixteenth century very little was left of any castle there might have been. The story is that Louis the Pious, son of Charlemagne, laid siege to Tourvéon to avenge the death of Roland. Ganelon, defeated and captured, was put in a barrel which had been hammered full of nails with their points projecting on the inside; the barrel was then rolled down the mountain. The Church of Chenelette is supposed to have been built at the point where it came to rest. Not far from here is Mont Saint-Rigaud, a place of pilgrimage which was formerly inhabited by a hermit rumoured to have special powers to remedy sterility in women.

But let us return to Beaujeu, whose centre is marked by an old half-timbered house opposite the Church of Saint-Nicolas. There is a legend attached to this place too. Apparently, up until the twelfth century, the valley was barred by a natural dam, upstream of which was a large lake. A son of the seigneur of Beaujeu, while hunting along its banks one day, slipped, fell into the water and drowned. The father wished to recover the body for Christian burial, but all attempts to find it were fruitless. Finally, the seigneur had the dam demolished and the lake drained; the corpse of the unfortunate youth was found at the bottom, and here the father built a church which has survived to this day.

You are now in the valley of the Ardières, which is the backbone of the historic Beaujolais. The Beaujeu family never inhabited the town proper, preferring to watch over it from their eyrie in the Château du Pierre Aigue, which dominates the entire valley. On each side of the river as it descends from Beaujeu to Belleville are *châteaux* which formerly belonged to the seigneur's vassals, strategically sited to guard the road.

ALONG THE ARDIÈRES

From Beaujeu, take the road which meanders along the left bank of the river. This will take you past Lantignié, then the *châteaux* of La Tour Bourdon and La Pierre. The latter belonged at one time to M Garnier, to whom is attributed the discovery of garnierite, the nickel ore of New Caledonia in the Pacific. The road continues to the Château de La Terrière, a charming manor house which was of considerable importance in the Middle Ages. The next landmark is the chapel of Saint-Ennemond, once a druidic holy place. Up until fairly recently, anxious mothers used to come here to scratch the miraculous stone supposed to cure unweaned babies of diarrhoea. The

Vats at Château de la Chaize

Château de la Chaize. (Naïve painting from the time when the château was being built, between 1674 and 1676)

seigneurs of Pizay, a square-towered stronghold nearby, were traditionally in the (profitable) business of protecting pilgrims. A little further on, still on the left bank of the river, stands the Château de L'Ecluse which guards the approaches to Belleville. This fourteenth-century fortress belonged to the Garadeur family, trusty knights in the service of the lords of Beaujeu.

The right bank of the Ardières has just as many castles as the left. At the head of Vallée du Samson is the well-preserved Château de Varennes, a reminder of the troubled times of the late sixteenth century when Frenchmen were killing each other wholesale for religious reasons. At that time M de Nagu-Varennes led the Catholics in the Lyonnais region, whilst M Barjot, who owned the

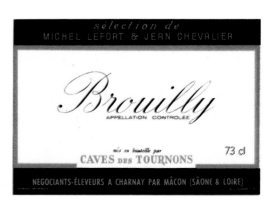

Château de La Palud, was a Protestant leader. The latter stronghold was only three or four kilometres distant from the former, which made for difficult local relations. Farther on from the Château de La Palud stands the Château de Saint-Lager, nestling in its village at the foot of the hill of Brouilly, yet which, along with its neighbour of Arginy, dominates the plain of the Saône. The Château d'Arginy is traditionally supposed to harbour the treasure of the Templars.

THE CELLARS OF LA CHAIZE

From Belleville, an excellent itinerary leads on to the Col de Poyebade. To reach this summit, the road ascends what might be called the sacred mountain of the Beaujolais, crowned with its chapel dedicated to Notre-Dame for her intercession against the plague of vine-mildew. The village of Odenas, through which the road passes, possesses more fermenting vats and a longer cellar than any other in the entire region. The cellar is no less than 105 metres long; while the vats belong to the Château de La Chaize. In the seventeenth century, the *château* was the property of the aristocratic Provençal family of La Chaize d'Aix. One of its members was Père La Chaize, Louis XIV's confessor, who gave his name to the famous cemetery in Paris. The *château* itself was designed and built by Mansard, while the French-style gardens were laid out by Lenôtre.

CLOCHEMERLE

Southward, along this road, is the small village of Saint-Etienne-La-Varenne, clustered on a peak around a charming little Romanesque church. Gallo-Roman tombs have been uncovered here and historians believe that Saint-Etienne was one of those fortified towns, well away from main lines of communication, used as sanctuaries by the inhabitants during the invasions of the third and fourth centuries. From here, the road continues along its winding way to Le Perréon and Vaux-en-Beaujolais.

Vaux prides itself on being the original of Gabriel Chevallier's *Clochemerle*, a novel eulogizing the earthiness, *joie de vivre* and good humour of country people. Vaux has also given its name to the river Vauxanne which begins here and winds peacefully down to join the Saône; but there is no wine grown here. Once you have crossed the 'Waters of the Vaux', a smaller road leads on to the village of Salles-en-Beaujolais, one of the area's great shrines, with its houses grouped around a magnificent Romanesque church and cloister. The latter were built by Cluniac monks, after the old Benedictine buildings and hospital on the island of Grelonges, on the Saône, were swept away by floods in 1300. The monks were later supplanted by nuns, on the orders of the Abbé de Cluny, and in the mid-eighteenth century the nuns were in turn replaced by canonesses when the convent became a chapter-house.

The aristocratic canonesses led a far more worldly life at Salles than their predecessors. Men were allowed to visit them – in all good faith – and many a love affair sprang up between them and the young daughters of noble families who came to finish their education under the canonesses'

Salles-en-Beaujolais: belltower and cloister

Withies for tying up the vines

watchful eye. As related in the foregoing chapter, it was thus that the Chevalier de Lamartine met and fell in love with Alix des Roys, while visiting his aunt the cannoness, Madame de Villars. The poet Alphonse de Lamartine was born of their union.

Take time to walk round the cloisters, where you can admire the fine stone carvings and the warm texture of the slightly ochred yellow masonry. This is surely a place filled with *douceur de vivre*.

FROM SAINT-JULIEN TO VILLEFRANCHE LA BELLE

Over the next hill, the soil changes colour completely: you are now in the district of Saint-Julien, where the earth is as red as the wine. This is the birthplace of Claude Bernard, the great medical pioneer, who often wrote to his dear friend and muse, Mme Raffalovitch, singing the praises of this landscape. The road proceeds southward, to the foothills of Mont Montmelas (*mons melas*, the black mountain), covered with pine woods and crowned by a chapel which, up till the Revolution, was a priory depending on the Abbey at Belleville. It later became one of the relay stations of the famous Chappe telegraph on the Paris–Marseilles line. On the side of the hill stands the massive Château de Montmelas, which was restored by a pupil of Viollet-Le-Duc. From here the road goes downwards to Villefranche. Slightly to the north is the commune of Arnas, where, on March 14, 1814, Marshall Augerau fought one of the last battles of the first campaign of France against an enemy four times superior in numbers.

Another period of conflict is recalled by the old church of Ouilly, nearby. In 1030, Fredelon, Vicomte d'Arnas, gave this church and its revenues to the Abbey of Savigny; this gift was contested by his daughter, the Abbess of Peloges, in the Ain region. Four years of guerilla warfare ensued, which culminated, of course, in an agreement.

The road has now brought you to Villefranche, the town which superceded Beaujeu as the capital of the province. It is worth entering the courtyards of some of Belleville's town houses, which recall the past splendour of this place during the fifteenth, sixteenth and eighteenth centuries. The people who lived here were always hard-working and cheerful, jealous of their independence and liberties; and if you take the time to look carefully and admire these old stones, they will reveal many hidden aspects of Belleville's history. While here, be sure to visit the collegiate church of Notre-Dame-des-Marais, an old building with an asymmetrical façade which boasts a magnificent Romanesque clocktower (east side) and a fifteenth-century Gothic façade (west side). This latter façade was bestowed on the church by Anne and Pierre de Beaujeu, who paid for it with fines imposed on the people of Trévoux, who had been caught making counterfeit coins.

THE PAYS DES PIERRES DORÉES

Leave the bustle of Belleville and drive away in the direction of Tarare; almost immediately you find yourself in quiet countryside once again. This area is known as the *Pays des Pierres Dorées*, the land of golden stone, because of the local building stone, a kind of yellow Jurassic chalk (Aalenian), which reflects the sunshine. The road leads past Liergues, with its fine Gothic church, to Pouilly-le-Monial which possesses a calvary with figures resembling those of Breton calvaries. North of Liergues are the commune of Gleizé and the Château de Vauxrenard. In the early nineteenth century, this *château* was used as a sanctuary by the Baron de

In the south of the Beaujolais

Richemont, who claimed that he was Louis XVII. Chervinges, nearby, has a charming Romanesque church.

Westward from Gleizé the road passes through Lacenas, with its little church of Sainte-Paule. Frescoes dating from the fourteenth century have recently been uncovered here. And not far off, on the banks of the river Morgon, stands the Château du Sou, which used to be one of the strongholds guarding the southern border of the Beaujolais; these were dependent on the Château de Montmelas.

THE TREASURE OF JARNIOUX

On the far side of the hill which rises south of Sou, the impressive and well-preserved Château de Jarnioux comes into sight. The village of the same name is tucked into a valley below the castle walls, and the surrounding mountains seem to protect it. Crowning one of these mountains is the Crêt du Py, a tumulus surrounded by stone sarcophagi, with the legend that a fabulous treasure is buried at the base of the natural theatre which has formed here. Apparently, if you can be on this spot on December 25, at the first stroke of midnight, the earth opens to reveal a brightly lit cave piled high with treasure. Yes, but . . . on the second stroke of midnight, the earth closes once again, and woe to anyone caught within; for he will remain there for ever. Not far from here is the little church of Saint-Clair, with stained glass windows excellently restored by Luc Barbier. A cluster of fine old Beaujolais houses stand around this church. From Saint-Clair, take the little road across the

ridges, which will bring you to Theizé. Here you will find the famous *bories*, or drystone shelters, whose age is an endless source of speculation. Though it is impossible to put a firm date on these odd vestiges, it is unlikely that they are prehistoric.

THE MUSCADINS OF THEIZÉ

The seventeenth-century ruined *château* of the Rochebonne family, an ancient fortified Romanesque church adjoining, and yellow chalk houses – these form the essence of Theizé, the little village from which *Le Président* Brossette wrote to his friend Boileau. In the past, Theizé distinguished itself rather disgracefully with its *Muscadins*, village-folk, who, in 1793, cut the throats of the Comte de Précy's troops as they escaped from the siege of Lyon. Having killed the fugitives, they stripped them of everything they possessed. For a long time afterwards, the *Muscadins* intermarried only amongst themselves, in order to preserve their secret and the booty their crime had brought them. But Theizé is also the village of the Château de Rapetour, and of Mme Roland's famous *Clos*, from which she was accustomed to write letters to her friends. Mme Roland passed many peaceful summers here before she went to Paris to open a salon and end her career on the scaffold.

From Theizé, continue to the old village of Oingt, with its spire and church tower proudly dominating the Azergues valley. The word Azergues is traditionally derived from the term *Oued Zerga* (blue water river) bestowed on it by Arab invaders in the early eighth century. Oingt itself is a very ancient village. Its feudal lord was very influential in the region. So much so that Renaud de Forez, Archbishop of Lyon, knowing him to be an ally of the Beaujeu family, was constrained to buy his neutrality with three loans of tens of thousands of gold pennies, *sous d'or*, a fortune at the time. Close to Oingt is the little manor of Prony, where the ghost of Claire de Saillans, a former lady of the manor, is said to walk at night, vainly searching for a peace

Pierres Dorées, *reflecting the light of the Beaujolais*

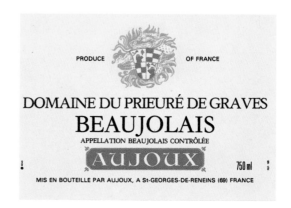

she will never find. On the hillside opposite stands the village of Sainte-Paule, which belonged to the Mont d'Or family in the Middle Ages. A branch of this family is said to have possessed the Horn of Roland, which was brought out and exhibited once a year at the monastery of Ile Barbe. The road continues into the valley, where it passes through Chamelet, a former castellany of the Beaujolais, with its old covered market, its venerable church, and the ruins of its castle. This place was a kind of locked gateway to the Beaujolais, astride the valley and squarely facing Ternand, the archbishop's township. It was also the home of M Riche, during the eighteenth century, who sought to buy a noble title by acquiring the post of Prosecutor at the Dombes Parliament. His son was the inventor of the hydraulic brake, drained the Pontin marshes, and was among those who founded the Ecole Polytechnique: for which he was made a baron by Louis XVIII.

THE LADY OF THE UNICORN

Heading back uphill to the plateau, the road passes through Bagnols. Unfortunately the towers of the Château de Bagnols have been demolished, but this stately old building still possesses one of the finest Gothic chimney pieces in the region. The *château* belonged to the seigneur Geoffroy de Roffec de Balzac, killed in battle in 1507; he left a widow, Claude Leviste, daughter of a Lyon alderman. Around 1511, she was courted by another nobleman, Adhémar de Chabannes de la Palisse (brother of the famous marshal of France who was 'still alive 15 minutes before his death'). Adhémar, nicknamed Le Petit Lion, is at the centre of the celebrated mystery of the *Dame à La Licorne*. At the Musée de Cluny, in Paris, there is a sequence of tapestries from the early eighteenth century which represent a lady accompanied by a unicorn. All the tapestries include armorial bearings of the Leviste family, but they are the arms of the male line, those of the female line being diamond-shaped. On each tapestry, in one of the lower

Among Jean-Charles Pivot's vines

BEAUJOLAIS

Sur mes lèvres ce sont trois syllabes qui chantent
Évoquant le vignoble aux pentes des coteaux;
Les villages coquets, les clochers, les châteaux,
Le silence et la paix de cloîtres qui m'enchantent.

Les corps noueux des ceps avec leurs échalas
Semblent de bons vieillards qui vont, courbant l'échine
Et s'aidant d'un bâton pour gravir la colline
Cheminent jour et nuit, sans jamais être las.

Des hauteurs de Brouilly, non loin de la chapelle,
J'embrasse du regard les centaines d'arpents
De rameaux emmêlés pareils à des serpents.
Pour eux, chaque saison tisse robe nouvelle.

Du bleu tendre à la pourpre et de l'or aux carmins,
Les pampres ne sont plus qu'une immense palette.
La Saône glisse au loin, longue couleuvre verte.
Déjà les vendangeurs sillonnent les chemins.

Les fruits mûrs tomberont coupés d'un geste agile
Dans les «jarlots» de bois bien propres au terroir.
Les grains s'écraseront sous le choc du pressoir,
Et le sang jaillira dans les cuves d'argile.

Le jus en fermentant dans l'ombre du tonneau
Dans son déchaînement bouillonnera de rage,
Dansera, bondira, mènera grand tapage,
Forgeant dans ses clameurs, l'âme du vin nouveau!...

Il a tous les reflets d'une naissante aurore,
Le discret velouté des trèfles incarnats,
Le rire du soleil l'irise de grenats
Quand dans le verre il roule en un glouglou sonore.

Il est toute allégresse, il est toute fraîcheur.
La pivoine, l'iris et la rose mourante,
La pêche, l'abricot, la groseille odorante
Se fondent pour créer sa typique saveur.

Il se rit des flacons habillés de poussière,
Des sommeils prolongés dans la nuit d'un caveau.
C'est un vin jeune et franc, gardant, tel un joyau,
La sève des sarments et les sucs de la terre.

Offrir une « tassée » est pour le vigneron
Le plus réconfortant souhait de bienvenue.
La rudesse de l'homme, un instant s'atténue.
Un attendrissement passe en ce gai luron.

Pour vanter son nectar aux vertus bienfaisantes :
Juliénas !... Saint-Amour !... Morgon !... Moulin-à-Vent !...
Noms fameux qu'il prononce avec un cœur fervent.
Beaujolais !... Beaujolais !... Trois syllabes qui chantent !...

R. MAUGER-KAUFFMANN
EXTRAIT DE L'*ALMANACH DU BEAUJOLAIS,* 1956

39

MORGON
APPELLATION MORGON CONTRÔLÉE

DOMAINE DES VERSAUDS

75 cl

SÉLECTIONNÉ ET MIS EN BOUTEILLES PAR
GEORGES DUBŒUF À 71720 ROMANÈCHE-THORINS, FRANCE
PRODUCED AND BOTTLED IN FRANCE

PRODUIT DE FRANCE
DOMAINE DE ROCHECORBIÈRE

Beaujolais

Appellation Beaujolais Contrôlée

750 ml

Alain Bidon, Viticulteur, 69 Chessy

MIS EN BOUTEILLE A LA PROPRIÉTÉ

Domaine du Martelat

M. DESSEIGNES   PROPRIÉTAIRE

BEAUJOLAIS·VILLAGES
APPELLATION BEAUJOLAIS-VILLAGES CONTRÔLÉE

CHER BEAUJOLAIS

Parmi les jolis coins de France,
Dont on célèbre les attraits,
Nous accordons la préférence
A notre pimpant Beaujolais.
Ses gaies et pittoresques lignes
Vont de la Saône jusqu'aux monts
Dominant ses coteaux de vignes
Et fermant ses doux horizons.

Tous ceux de nous qu'il a vus naître
Lui gardent leur fidélité;
D'autres sont venus le connaître
Et, sans retour, l'ont adopté.
C'est ainsi que les uns, les autres,
Nous demeurons ses vrais enfants;
De ses vertus faisons les nôtres
Et célébrons-les dans nos chants :

« Nous t'apprécions, cher pays,
« Tu plais à tous car tu souris;
« Ton charme sait réjouir l'âme
« Comme une claire et douce flamme;
« Et nous conservons la gaîté
« En buvant ton vin réputé,
« Élixir de longévité,
« Puisque la joie c'est la santé ! »

JEAN LAPLANCHE
EXTRAIT DE L'*ALMANACH DU BEAUJOLAIS*, 1955

corners, a tiny lion has been embroidered. Were these famous tapestries a gift from Adhémar de Chabannes to his fiancée, Claude, with whom he later enjoyed four years of marriage before dying, like his predecessor, in combat for the King of France? No one has ever been able to answer this question. As for Geoffroy, the first husband, he lies buried in the chapel of the Château de Châtillon d'Azergues, an odd two-storey building attached to the old fortress.

On the way to Bagnols is the little mining village of Chessy. The copper mines here have been worked since Gallo-Roman times. No less a figure than the great financier, Jacques Cœur, formed a partnership with a baronet of Lyon to extract the maximum profit from Chessy in the mid-fifteenth century. At one stage of the diggings, a very fine vein of copper carbonate was discovered, which had the property of crystallizing into balls. This was named Chessylite, after Chessy. The fifteenth-century village church is also well worth a visit – it has been suggested that Jacques Cœur and his wife are depicted in one of the windows. There is a steep path leading from here to the Château des Chanoines-Comptes de Lyon, but if you choose to linger in the little streets of Chessy, you will find they offer many intriguing details of mediaeval architecture.

THE AZERGUES

Follow the road along the river Azergues as far as Chazay, once the seat of the Abbots of Ainay. It was here that the Abbé du Terrail received his nephew, Bayard, the day after his first victory in a tournament at Lyon. Chazay is also associated with the legendary Babouin, a brave bear-tamer who scaled the blazing tower of the *château* to save the owner's daughter from the flames. He succeeded in bringing the girl down unharmed and was (of course) rewarded with her hand in marriage; his statue still adorns the ramparts. The palace of the Abbots of Ainay still remains at Chazay, along with several fifteenth- and sixteenth-century houses and part of the town's old fortifications. Northward from here is Morance, with its Romanesque church. There is a suggestion that the name of this

SAINT-LAURENT-D'OINGT.

village originated with the Moors, since some of the capitals in the apse include black faces. Before the Revolution the parish belonged to the Dames de Saint-Pierre, a Benedictine order based at the Place des Terreaux in Lyon. From here, the road climbs to Charnay at the top of a hill looking out on one side across the Saône valley and on the other towards the woodlands of Alix. The commune of Charnay possesses a quarry which has yielded a number of remarkable fossils; a twelve-metre-long ichthyosaur was unearthed here recently. Near this quarry is the old Château de Bayères. A spring at Bayères used to be famous for the delicious taste of its water. According to legend, a brigand was once put to the water torture here; after the wretch had been made to swallow two bucketfuls, the funnel was taken from his mouth and he was asked if he had anything to say. 'Yes', he replied. 'Give me more!' Altogether, Charnay's old church, its tastefully preserved *château*, its two-metre-high statue of Saint Roch and its houses built of *pierres dorées* offer a most attractive architectural ensemble.

THE ERA OF CUT STONE

The road winds on from Charnay to Alix, on the west side of the hill. Here there used to be a chapter house, to which Mme de Genlis was sent, when she was fifteen, to finish her education. This lady was later to entrance Philippe Egalité with her knowledge of the arts of love, before being supplanted, in the prince's bed, if not in his heart, by Mme Buffon. During the Middle Ages, there was a

Benedictine convent at Alix.
Although, curiously enough, the nuns
habitually went to the Abbey of
Savigny (an all male institution) to
take their vows. After the Revolution,
the chapter was transformed into a
seminary by Cardinal Fesch, and
today it is an old people's home. Just
off the road, on the other side of Alix,
are the scattered remains of the
château which once belonged to the
Marze family, trusty henchmen of the
house of Beaujeu.

The next village is Lachassagne,
fief of the Mortemart dynasty. The
white wines of Lachassagne are
famous locally. During the eighteenth
century, people used to come here
from Lyon to indulge – or as the
phrase went, 'to take the waters at
Lachassagne'. The village stands

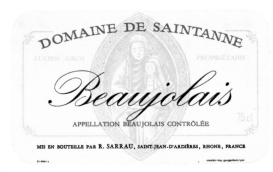

VAUX-EN-BEAUJOLAIS

NOTRE-DAME-DES-MARAIS A VILLEFRANCHE.

astride a ridge that stretches from Limas to Belmont. This ridge, which is chiefly composed of Jurassic chalk, is unique in that its oldest strata are on the surface and its most recent ones buried below. In other words, the terrain is upside down. The fracture that caused this geological freak is clearly visible as the Merloup valley; the result is a surface zone which is particularly rich in silex deposits. At Le Campinien, between Alix and Lachassagne, there used to be a number of stone-built factories producing assorted arms and tools.

THE OVENS AT ANSE

From Lachassagne, the road drops down towards the Saône valley, via Anse, which was once a Gallo-Roman *castrum*. The walls (third–fourth century) are still visible, surfaced with hand-cut stone. West of the *castrum* stands the fortress erected by Archbishop Renaud de Forez in the thirteenth century, with its two massive keeps. Anse, which originally belonged to the canons of Lyon, is famous for the oven that was once operated here on the principle that every customer brought his own dough to make his own bread. The man who tended the oven would take a handful of dough as payment, and the housewives would wait on the premises till their loaves were baked. The story goes that these ladies would pass the time by challenging any passing male to prove his virility on the spot; if he failed to do so, he received the same treatment as Abelard. There is even a rumour that an archbishop was put to this exacting test. To this day, the people

of Anse refer to a woman of doubtful virtue as having passed '*devant le four*', ('in front of the oven').

Do not leave Anse without making a foray across the Saône to visit the old Château de Saint-Bernard, another stronghold which formerly belonged to the canons of Lyon, and the delightful little Gothic church opposite. Suzanne Valadon lived for years in this *château* with Utter and her son Utrillo. Today it is the property of M Lafoy.

THE BANKS OF THE SAÔNE

From Anse, take the RN6 northward past Villefranche. Beside the Saône, the Château de Boistrait stands guarding the Gué de Grelonges, a much frequented pass in Roman times. Further on is the large market town of Saint-Georges-de-Reneins, clustered around its Romanesque church. If you take the road to Montmerle, you will see the Marze family's small moated manor house. When you reach Belleville again, spare some time to visit the lovely collegiate church. This pure Romanesque building was completed in eleven years by Humbert III of Beaujeu. The seventeenth-century hospital nearby still has quarters set aside for old people, in imitation of the Hospices de Beaune. There is a single difference: the rooms at Belleville are still in use.

The road has now gone nearly full circle, back to the boundary stone mentioned at the start of this chapter. The final stretch leads past d'Ardières, with the Château de l'Ecluse nestled in woodlands close by. Turn left by the Voisin

monument for a visit to the well-preserved mediaeval Château de Corcelles; or, if you prefer, take the right fork to Drace, whose Romanesque church was ceded to the Abbey of Savigny around 1030. Here the tour ends. I have made no mention of monuments and beauty spots, but I hope that this brief outline will sharpen the visitor's curiosity and encourage him to make his own explorations.

BEAUJOLAIS-VILLAGES

Appellation Beaujolais-Villages Contrôlée

Mis en bouteille à F 69205 Belleville-s/-Saône pour Pieroth Frères et Fils
Négociants-Eleveurs au Cuvage des Pierres à Saint-Amour (S.-&-L.)

Le Cuvage des Pierres

75 cl e

Signé à l'Attention Exclusive de nos Fidèles Clients

MORGON

APPELLATION CONTROLÉE

75 cl

Mis en bouteille par THORIN F 71570 PONTANEVAUX

Georges GRUAT

The Beaujolais was in a desperate state. Domestic animals wandered aimlessly by the roadsides, driven out by their owners who no longer had food for them. Imagine, the wine-growers of the Beaujolais, a race renowned for their hospitality, beating their livestock from their doors like barbarians! These were the scenes described in the journal *Lyon Viticole* in 1880.

At that time, wine was vanishing from cafés and restaurants all over France; down in the *Rouge Midi*, people were up in arms against bootleggers peddling moonshine made from industrial alcohol. The Beaujolais had also tried to formulate some kind of collective protest, but in the end the wine-growers were forced to desert their vineless properties and make their way to the cities in search of work. Anything rather than die of despair beside vineyards being devoured before their eyes by billions of aphids, the dreaded phylloxera from America. Older men in the north of the region could still remember the 'endless winter' of fifty years before, when another plague had struck the Romanèche, Chénas and Saint-Amour areas. At that time, the temptation to burn the infested vines had been very strong; there seemed to be no other way of fighting the wretched pyralis. A storm struck the procession of boats across the Saône and quickly turned the pilgrimage to Notre-Dame du Ver

into a catastrophe; it looked as if even heaven had abandoned them. But then Benoît Raclet, in his little house at Romanèche-Thorins, stumbled on the simplest of remedies for pyralis: that of spraying the vines with boiling water during the winter. To begin with, Raclet was accused of witchcraft, but the evidence of his success soon proved irrefutable. The storehouses of the region, which for fifteen years had held only a few miserable quarter casks, once again were redolent with the good smell of Beaujolais wine.

After pyralis, phylloxera. It was written, said some, in Genesis, the

first book of the Bible: 'Thou shall plant thy vine and cultivate it, but no wine shall thou drink, for the worms shall consume it'. Why struggle against the will of the Lord? But Victor Pulliat, an ampelographer living at Chiroubles and son of a wine-grower, refused to listen to such nonsense. He decided to wage total war against the epidemic. Pulliat conducted a series of experiments, pooled his results with those of other researchers like Millardet, Vialla and Planchon, and one day discovered that phylloxera could be overcome by grafting on to American rootstock. This breakthrough gave new hope to the wine-growers, who wished only to live on their land according to the cycle of the seasons. The work might be hard and thankless, but they loved their vines like their own children.

The Beaujolais took twenty years to recover from the devastation of phylloxera. And then, quite suddenly, the region found itself crushed by overproduction. The 1900 harvest yielded 200 hectolitres per hectare, leading to a collapse in prices. The value of the harvested grapes was so low that it was uneconomical to pick them. The system had to be completely reorganized all over again, and at the same time a host of new diseases had to be faced: mildew, oidium, black rot, grey rot . . . Nothing was ever certain. Generation followed generation, each adding its own contribution to the structure of the Beaujolais. Thousands of wine-growers still carried out the same ancestral work, but now modern techniques made it possible for one dedicated man to work six hectares of vines on his own. (Prior to the First World War, the maximum had been two and a half hectares.) Furthermore, an organized professional structure was now in place to handle the marketing of Beaujolais as a highly appreciated wine. As Louis Orizet said, the region had 'deserved its victory'. But let us

The wine-grower's verdict

now turn to the vineyards and the men of today's Beaujolais.

PLANTING A BEAUJOLAIS VINEYARD

The black Gamay grape, with its clear white juice, was rejected in the seventeenth century by the aldermen of Mâcon. Its revenge was swift, for this vine was found to be equally at home both in the clay-lime of the southern Beaujolais and in the granitic soil of the north. But the Gamay is also extremely demanding. It needs ground that is free of threadworms and root remains. Before the appearance of agricultural chemicals, the only way this could be achieved was by resting the soil for five years. Since the wine-growers had to make some kind of living in the meantime, it was common practice to turn out dairy cattle on the fields for the five-year period. This practice also offered a margin of profit from milk sales when wine prices were depressed.

Thus, for many years, wine and milk were the staples of the Beaujolais region; and indeed it was a Beaujolais wine-grower, Benoît Aurion, who created the basic milk-marketing organization of all France. Today, economic changes have banished the dairy cow from the Beaujolais and the soil is now disinfected more rapidly by a fumigation process. But the land must first be sub-soiled, a back-breaking job facetiously known as mine clearance, *déminage*. This operation has changed considerably over the years.

At the beginning of the century, there was no alternative to the spade; but it took plenty of sweat to sub-soil one hectare to a depth of twenty-five centimetres. When animal draught methods appeared around 1912, the older inhabitants could scarcely believe their eyes. Beside themselves with rage, they fumed that horse, men and plough would all drop down dead – but, nonetheless, the method proved much less exhausting and the poorest wine-growers, who couldn't afford horses, harnessed their cows to the plough. Then came mechanization; winches were used for the steepest inclines, along with the famous double-furrow trenching ploughs, *charrues dauphinoises*.

In the classic process of preparation, when the sub-soiling is finished, the ground is rolled and the clods are broken up, as for an ordinary seedbed. It is much improved thereby and is ready to receive grafted rootstock which will have nothing to fear from phylloxera.

But the wine-grower's trials are not yet at an end. Now he has to set to with the dibber, *plantoir*, and dig 10,000 holes per hectare to plant his vines – more expenditure of effort. Meanwhile, in the laboratories, oenologists and technicians seek to perfect planting methods while lightening the wine-grower's labours – with such innovations as the grafted plant in its pot, to be placed directly in the soil surrounded with its own chunk of turf.

After planting, it takes four years before the first grapes are harvested in an *appellation d'origine controlée* (guaranteed vintage). But all through those years the vines must be taken care of: they have to be treated against mildew and oidium from the first year onward; then propped with stakes, *palissage*; then treated again to ward off fruitworm.

PRUNING POINTS

The benefits of chemistry cannot be praised enough, for the use of weedkillers has totally changed viticultural methods. No longer does the earth around vines have to be ridged up after the harvest is over and no longer does the piled soil have to be cleared away from the plants prior to pruning. The hoe has been virtually superannuated. The

panniers which were formerly used to bring earth up into the vineyards are now relegated to the status of old-fashioned accessories.

Yet the wine-grower himself is by no means inactive. The disappearance of his old chores has come hand in hand with a new need for him to cultivate as much land as possible in order to earn a decent living. And no machine will ever be invented to replace the human hand in the matter of pruning vines. . . .

A grafting workshop

Domaine du Clos Verdy

Chiroubles

APPELLATION CHIROUBLES CONTROLÉE

Mise en Bouteilles au Domaine   750 ML

Georges BOULON, Viticulteur - 69115 Chiroubles
PRODUCE OF FRANCE

BOUTEILLE
Nº 792269

La Cornaline

CHENAS
APPELLATION CHENAS CONTROLÉE

mis en bouteilles par   75 cl

J.-C. OLLIVON
NÉGOCIANT-ÉLEVEUR A ROMANÈCHE-THORINS (SAONE-ET-LOIRE)
BEUVERY - BEAUNE

CHATEAU DES GRANGES
BEAUJOLAIS

APPELLATION BEAUJOLAIS CONTROLÉE
Comte H. de RAMBUTEAU, Propriétaire

MIS EN BOUTEILLE PAR   THORIN   F 71570 PONTANEVAUX
Produce of France
37,5cl

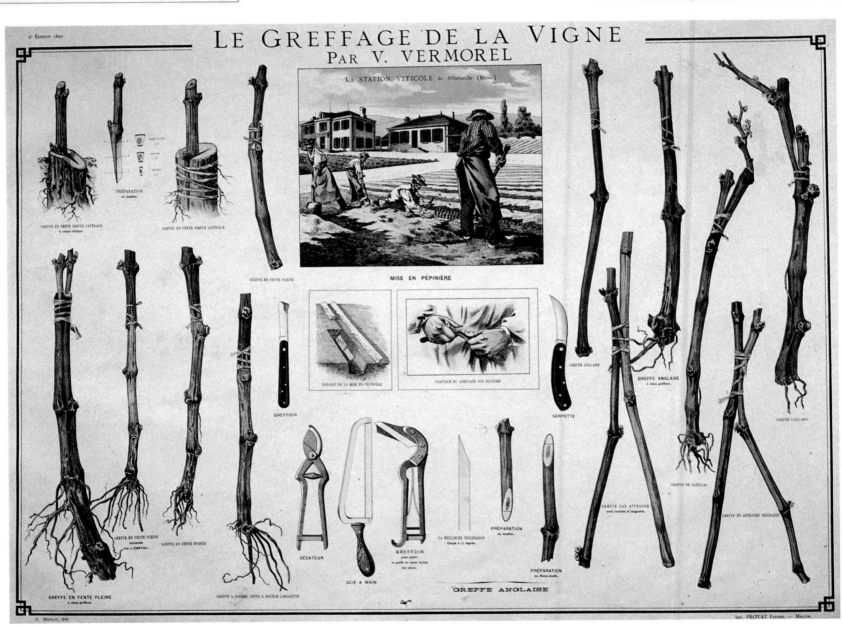

VIN DE FRANCE

DOMAINE DE LA CHIZE

Beaujolais-Villages

APPELLATION BEAUJOLAIS-VILLAGES CONTROLÉE   75 cl
MIS EN BOUTEILLE DANS LA RÉGION DE PRODUCTION PAR

J. PELLERIN - SAINT-GEORGES-DE-RENEINS (RHÔNE) FRANCE

"CUVÉE DAILLY"
BEAUJOLAIS BLANC
APPELLATION BEAUJOLAIS BLANC CONTROLÉE

MIS EN BOUTEILLE A LA CHAPELLE-DE-GUINCHAY PAR LE

CLUB FRANÇAIS DU VIN   75 cl
LANCIÉ (RHONE) 69220

Beaujolais-Villages

APPELLATION CONTROLÉE   75cl

Réserve du Gouverneur Militaire de Lyon

ORANGE DOUBLE EFFET

ÉCLAIR Nº 1

TRIPLEX

BLOIS

JUPITER

NABO

During the long autumn and winter months, the wine-grower must work outside in his vineyard, despite the cold which numbs and swells his fingers in the morning mist. And pruning is no easy matter; it requires long experience and a deep knowledge of vines. The plant must be coaxed to produce its best; at the same time its twelve 'eyes', or pruning points, must be retained, since twelve 'eyes' are the maximum allowable for the vintage. But pruning must also be carried out with a view to what is planned for the following year. In many respects, the harvest depends on efficient pruning methods. For months on end, the wine-grower has to stay stooped in the most back-breaking of postures, tirelessly squeezing away at his secateurs. This is a terrible chore that no technician or academic will ever succeed in eliminating. It constitutes the tribute which must be paid to the land by men and women who live in partnership with nature. Recently, an inventive Quincié wine-grower named Jean-Charles Pivot (brother of the French TV personality Bernard Pivot) invented a chair which takes away some of the back pain from which all his colleagues suffer. But never presume to call the other M Pivot an 'armchair pruner'! . . .

SUMMER IN THE VINEYARD

When spring comes, *le printemps en fleur qui sur ses pantoufles brille*, as Verlaine puts it, the vine begins to sprout and sprawl vigorously. It must be soothed and to this purpose the sterile buds which produce over-abundant foliage are cut back. This process is called trimming, *émondage*.

At this stage, the vine is as fragile as a baby and requires enormous care. From the beginning of spring until the grapes are ripe, it is a constant prey to mildew. This disease, like the rootstock of modern vines, originally came from America. The spraying of a copper sulphate solution, *bouillie bordelaise*, has so far held mildew in check, and remains *de rigueur* in spite of other progress in the field. But other assorted fungi and insects still threaten, such as oidium,

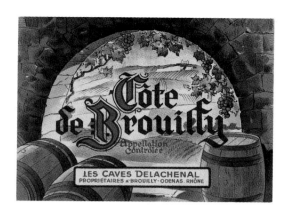

SULFATAGES

Divisé par le jet, le sulfate cuisant
En pleuvant sur les ceps rejaillit et crépite :
Innombrables versets que la vigne récite,
En jetant son parfum en offrande au printemps.

Ainsi, sur le satin des feuilles ponctuées,
Que ne rongera plus le mal insidieux,
Se posent, au hasard, par légères nuées,
De frêles oiselets et des papillons bleus.

PIERRE AGUÉTANT
EXTRAIT DU *POÈME DU BEAUJOLAIS*, 1922

55

a real scourge to the wine-growers of former times who built the chapel of Notre-Dame de Brouilly to protect against it; black rot, which produces lesions; leaf-devouring red spiders; and, finally, grey rot, a fungus which attacks the grapes.

For more than six months of the year the wine-grower is engaged in a ceaseless struggle, scrupulously observing the advice of technicians for each treatment of his vines. And this chemical warfare is expensive, though its techniques have evolved over the years. The first back-pack sprayers were manufactured in the factories of a Villefranche industrialist named Victor Vermorel. Compressors appeared during the 1950s. These contraptions completely changed spraying methods and were a great boon to all viticulturists.

Sans crainte de pressoir, le pampre tout l'été
Boit les doux présents de l'Aurore.
(All summer long, the vine branch drinks
the dawn's soft dew, and never dreads the press.)

The vine flowers at the same time as the lily; a hundred days later, the start of the grape harvest will be proclaimed. This is an anxious moment for the wine-grower, who during this period is completely at the mercy of the elements.

Meanwhile the vine grows and grows, spreading out over the ground 'like a cat on heat' as the French

Scalding the vines (pastel from the Musée Raclet)

phrase goes. It must be lifted and tied up with withies, so that it can keep its queenly carriage and avoid being crushed by the wheels of the tractor moving along the rows. This is a long job which involves the whole family, boys and girls included.

The weather can never be counted on, given the constant threat of hail. Many a wine-grower has watched helplessly, with tears in his eyes, as the hailstones slash down, ripping foliage to shreds, bruising grapes and tearing the wood from the vines. What can be done? Nothing. Every possible solution has been attempted in the Beaujolais. The effect of

prayers having proven strictly relative, bells were rung when hail threatened. Then cannons and rockets were tried, to no avail: the hail still came down.

After a series of particularly violent storms, a defence association was formed, which decided to take extreme measures and use aeroplanes to spray the stormclouds with silver iodide. There was something to be said for this system, but it would have required the use of dozens of aircraft. As Papa Bréchard commented, 'Maybe we should go back to prayers. At least they wouldn't cost so much.'

Thus the Beaujolais abandoned the idea of aerial defence against hail, but not before some local wags had persuaded a young journalist, on the look-out for a story, that the most effective Beaujolais preventive was the systematic painting of each vineleaf with silver iodide. When the newspaper was shown to President Lavarenne, he nearly choked to death.

Finding themselves unable to defend their vines, the wine-growers of the Beaujolais decided at least to defend their revenues. They therefore invented a 'hail insurance' system, based on solidarity – the only one in France.

THE GRAPE HARVEST

Down on the *autoroute*, on the eastern edge of the Beaujolais, the holidaymakers are roasting in their

cars. The long ribbon of traffic undulates like the wave of conscripts from Villefranche, but no wine-grower would dream of joining it. For him, the holiday period is the time when he puts the finishing touches to his vines: the paring, *rognage*, which he does twice with his shears, to cut out over-abundant foliage.

Summer sinks into September, with its dust-clouds and morning mists. . . .

This is the most critical moment of the year. The right moment must be chosen to proclaim the beginning of the harvest, the right day selected for each patch of vines, according to the state of the grapes and the results of tests carried out by the technicians. In spite of many worries still to come, the harvest brings the wine-grower's reward. *Allez Pierette, va prendre ta serpette!* In the old days, when the vineyards were relatively small, most of the labour of harvesting fell to the wine-grower's families and immediate neighbours. A helping hand with the grapes, as with the corn at threshing time, was paid for by a good meal and reciprocated during the neighbour's harvest. The owners of large vineyards went down to the village square where harvesters could be hired every morning. Hard bargains were driven over the price of a day's work, but the men selling their services were grafters who thought nothing of starting at dawn to put in a twelve- or fourteen-hour day among the vines.

Between the wars, when the vineyards were beginning to develop and expand, the Beaujolais discovered the mining folk of Montceau-les-Mines. These people were mostly Polish by origin, deep drinkers but good workers; they spent their holidays (paid for by the Socialist Popular Front) harvesting grapes in the Beaujolais. In each 'cut', '*coupée*' (ie group of twelve workers harvesting one hectare in a day), blond, laughing girls from the Polish black country stood picking grapes and singing ditties from their faraway homeland. They would only straighten their backs to call out *jarlot!* for the vat carrier when their buckets were full.

In the 1960s the Beaujolais went through a period when harvesters were scarce. There were no job-seekers to be found jostling around the doors of town halls, as in the euphoric days of 'economic expansion'. . . .

Then came the students, mostly foreign, who were attracted by the promise of 'first-hand experience of the working world'. With their long hair and their guitars slung over their shoulders, they came down to the Beaujolais to sample the wine-grower's warm hospitality and the solid early-morning snack, *casse-croûte*. And yesterday's hippies have become today's friends. The wine-growers remain much attached to student labour, which is now all the more loyal since many owners have fixed up comfortable lodgings with

A hail cannon

complete sanitary facilities for their temporary guests.

The grape harvest also attracts other less welcome types of worker: tramps, vagrants, down and outs and fugitives from justice wishing to remain anonymous. These characters usually only work for a single day before moving on; they rarely find a job in a proper band of harvesters. Not surprisingly, the *gendarmes* tend to keep a close eye on the vineyards at this period of the year. For example, in the last century a man named David was arrested at Saint-Jean-des-Vignes, who had quietly attached himself to the grape harvesters. He turned out to be one of the celebrated *chauffeurs de la Drôme*, a band of vicious murderers. His fellow workers must have had the cold shivers when the truth was known.

Adieu paniers, vendages sont faites, said Rabelais. But before the workers go their separate ways, the traditional *revole* must be held, a copious end-of-harvest meal punctuated with much singing and dancing in the old style.

Unquestionably, new methods of culture and the evolution of sophisticated machinery have enabled the Beaujolais to change its status from *petit vin de comptoir* to that of a great vintage. But the benefits of machinery can surely be pushed even further. For example, why not mechanize the grape harvest, which is presently so expensive, and causes such difficulties in terms of administrative worries and short-term accommodation for workers?

Well . . . this is a sensitive point. The younger people gaze longingly at the new harvesting machines – not just the wine-growers who are firm converts to mechanization anyway, but also their wives, the cooks, who never seem to have big enough saucepans to feed all those mouths.

So the Beaujolais has been making experiments . . . which so far have been inconclusive. Polite suggestions have been made to manufacturers that machines be adapted to suit the wine-making techniques of the Beaujolais. But at the same time the various heads of viticultural organizations have requested the INAO to publish a decree stipulating that grapes in the Beaujolais should be 'harvested whole', that is, undamaged; a neat twist, which has the effect of prohibiting machine harvesting, without banning it. *Allez Pierrette . . . tu reprendras ta serpette!* In the Beaujolais, the festival of the grape harvest still has every chance of going on for ever.

HEAVEN BOUND

By October's end,
the grapes are in the vat . . .

The vats are ready. All the pipes and recipients have been sterilized. The wine-grower is fully aware that the success of the vinification process chiefly depends on this meticulous pre-harvest work.

At the height of the harvest, the wine-grower metamorphoses into an alchemist, with Beaujolais as his philosopher's stone. It is vital that the grapes arrive in the vats uncrushed, if his wines are to retain their originality – which is why he has rejected the siren call of excessive

mechanization. There's no secret about winemaking in the Beaujolais; you only need to obey the rules.

Nonetheless, the most anxious moment of all comes when the grapes are fermenting in the vats. Twice a day, the wine-grower regulates the fermentation and warms or cools the vats according to the prevalent climatic conditions. Fundamentally, nothing has changed, except that modern equipment is much more trustworthy than the old techniques, which involved listening carefully to the various stages of fermentation and shifting wine from one vat to another to speed (or slow) the process.

The advent of the mustimeter made it possible to choose the correct moment for racking the wine. Formerly, the wine-growers used to wait till the must was no longer covered before racking; this procedure was very rough and ready, even though the old method of judgement by the cupful, *tasse*, has a certain nostalgic appeal.

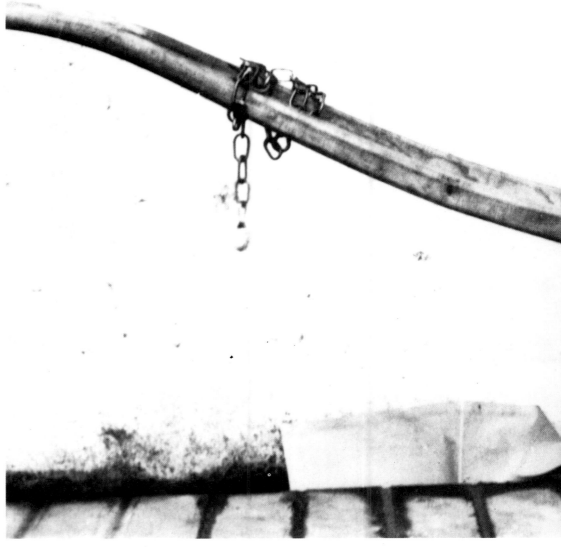

There is no question that the work of technicians and researchers has been very useful in relieving the anxieties of the wine-grower and in greatly improving the quality of the wine. Chaptalization is a technique which has been greatly developed by research and enough nonsense has been said and written about it to fill a book.

The adversaries of chaptalization view it from one angle only: the fact that industrial sugar is added to the must in order to produce more alcohol. Thus, according to them, the wine is denatured. What actually happens is the opposite: chaptalization in the vat, by raising the degree of alcohol, enables tannins and colouring agents to dissolve more readily.

The oenologists, whom nobody can accuse of incompetence, are categorical on this point. . . .

'The addition of sucrose restarts fermentation and contributes to the development of glycerine and other secondary substances produced by fermentation. It contributes to the diminution of acidity by the precipitation of part of the solution of bitartrate of potassium in the wine. Hence chaptalization should not be considered as a practice whose sole purpose is to raise the alcohol content of wine. It improves its savour, by which is meant the impression of body and fullness that it gives.'

I once gave a non-chaptalized Beaujolais to an opponent of the practice. He concluded that the wine was not a Beaujolais at all – and this from a man who liked to boast that he was the equal of many professional tasters and who said he only cared for the Petit Beaujolais of pre-war times. But here let us close this brief technical digression.

The wine-grower goes to his wine-
    press
as a priest goes to his altar.

The first pressing is always a ceremonial occasion. Of course, the old treadmill has vanished, with its husky lads vying to show off their strength to the young maidens waiting for the *paradis* – those first sweet drops which must be caught up

instantly and tasted, like the scent of roses, before they vanish. Nowadays, vineyards are equipped with horizontal presses, but the ceremony of the pressing still has its ritual integrity. It embodies the miracle of a safely gathered harvest and the *paradis* opens the doors of ecstasy.

The wine lying in the vat is like a newborn baby in its cradle. It must be jealously cared for and its alcoholic fermentation must be carefully regulated. Ten, sometimes twenty times a day, the wine-grower will go with his *tasse* from one vat to another; his palate infallibly follows the slow transformation of sugar into alcohol and the appearance of the perfumes that are characteristic of Beaujolais. Millions of loyal amateurs all over the world are waiting for this wine. But, before it is delivered up to the greedy hordes, the Beaujolais must do its *malo*, a local term for malolactic fermentation, or conversion of malic acid into lactic acid.

After this, the wine can be submitted to the popular judgement. Each year, it receives its quota of unexpected compliments:

– *Il est coquin, amuseur, un rien espiegle.*
(Cheeky, entertaining, a trifle mischievous.)
– *C'est un polisson, canaille en diable!*
(A scamp, with a wicked twinkle . . .)
– *Ah, mes amis, c'est le petit Jésus qui vous glisse dans le gosier en culottes de velours.*
(Like the baby Jesus, slipping down your gullet in velvet trousers . . .)
– *Et cette robe, regardez cette robe, c'est celle d'une princesse!*
(And look at that colour! fit for a princess . . .)

The grape harvest at Saint-Etienne-La-Varenne

Before the tractors came

– Et quelle grâce!
(And what charm . . .)
– Quel parfum! Ca, c'est pas du pathchouli!
(And what a perfume! No mere patchouli* that!

All these adjectives go out in television, radio and press agency reports, to the great delight of the wine-growers. One pen-pusher even discovered that a certain vintage had the thighs of a Bluebell Girl . . .

But I am inclined to think that Beaujolais, with all the sweat and veneration it inspires, simply has a taste of love.

*Patchouli is a well-known cheap perfume.

HISTORY IS MADE BY MEN

For today's observer, everything seems simple. The wine-grower makes a quality product, the wine-merchant adds the finishing touches, professional organizations arrange for good publicity, the Beaujolais establishes a solid reputation and its solidarity is quoted as an example to other regions. But before this stage was reached, many barriers had to be broken down and many battles had to be won. Many wine-growers, wine-merchants, technicians and ordinary citizens of the Beaujolais fought bitterly for decades to make their region what it is. Their names don't figure in *Who's Who* or the *Almanach de Gotha* and most of them are forgotten. But their work remains; probably this was their sole ambition. Patience and hard work win through! From the eighteenth century

BEAUJOLAIS . . . AND COCA-COLA

Propaganda on behalf of our Beaujolais wines is still a necessity. All our producers are convinced of this. They are not oblivious to the recent inroads made by certain expandable soft drinks from America which are attempting to gain a foothold in French establishments. Compulsive advertising is being carried out on behalf of American Coca-Cola. Trucks plastered with multi-coloured posters have been seen moving along the main arterial road leading across our Beaujolais hillsides. This fizzy water, with one or two additives which give it a bittersweet taste and certain stimulating qualities; this soft drink taken with ice . . . surely, you will say, it cannot seriously compete with our pots de Beaujolais! But beware! We are talking about advertising and modern trends! Even the name of Coca-Cola has attractive overtones of fun and gaiety. The product is cheap. It's unlikely to be drunk with a good sausage, a roast chicken, or a well-cooked piece of game. But we should beware of it taking over in our cafés and bistros, where the drinking of Beaujolais, and often of vintage Beaujolais, is still so popular. Cafés and bistros are the most important outlets for our wines. A simple cry of alarm — but let's remember how it was with cocktails, toffee apples and chewing-gum.

Extract from the *Almanach du Beaujolais*, 1950.

onwards, the wines of the Beaujolais were brought down to the Loire along the Beaujeu–Charlieu road. From Charlieu they were shipped to Paris. Their fame had gone out well beyond the borders of the Lyonnais region, and the men of the Beaujolais combined with their colleagues from other areas to press for recognition of the principle of *appellation d'origine contrôlée*. As the creole proverb goes, '. . . with a little patience, a man can pluck the feathers off eggs.' Wine-

growers, as a race, are both patient and tenacious. The twentieth century finally ushered in the era of the *appellation d'origine contrôlée*, with the people of the Beaujolais in the thick of all the negotiations that ensued. The first official texts on the matter sought to protect the *appellation d'origine*, but the law of 1905 did no more than set administrative limits to the vineyard areas. Few people on the spot took much notice of this, since none of the technical aspects of winemaking had

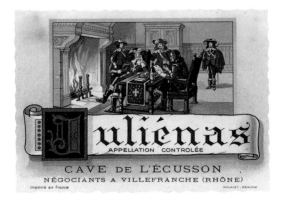

yet been addressed, and the 1905 law was completely ineffectual. Nevertheless, one of its provisions still remains in force: the *Service des Fraudes!* For the following reasons: at the turn of the century, the vineyards were still being rebuilt after the invasion of phylloxera. As an encouragement to production, the government advocated the addition of sugar to the wine on a massive scale. As much as twenty-five gold francs per quintal of sugar were offered as a subsidy. The result was a gold rush. Never was so much jam made in France's winemaking regions as in the early years of the twentieth century. In order to restore the sugar to its original destination, authorities were forced to set up obligatory inspections of vats.

The subsidies disappeared a long time ago, only to be replaced by a tax on the sugar used for chaptalization. But the inspections have outlasted successive new laws and governments, just like the *Service de la Répression des Fraudes* . . . the French administration doesn't surrender its prerogatives easily. In 1919, a new law was passed. This too failed. The boundaries of the 'appellations' were no longer an administrative matter, but a judicial one. However, the true Frenchman is a past master at exploiting legislative loopholes. At that time the wine industry was in crisis. Dearth had been followed by abundance . . . and the government had established taxes on wines, but only on everyday wines: *appellations d'origine* were therefore exempted. Hence the new law did not apply to production norms; it concerned only geographic ones. The result was a sudden proliferation of new *appellations*.

The law had other flaws, even after its amendment in 1927 which specified that both land and vine varieties had to be sanctioned by 'local, honest and consistent' practices. However, the wine-growers were in no haste to obtain judicial definitions of their vine varieties and areas of production. They even tried to hoodwink the magistrates with 'agreement suits', whereby they would bring mutual actions in order to acquire *appellations*. In the Beaujolais, a Chénas wine-grower, M

Méziat, concluded that while the law had many failings, it did at least offer wine producers a means of operating as an entity – no longer in commune-based unions, but under the banner of a single *appellation*. Most of the Chénas wine-growers rallied to Méziat's cause, as did those of Romanèche-Thorins in the neighbouring area of Saône-et-Loire.

'We all have the same granitic, manganese-enriched soil. We all have the same vine variety. So let's unite and sell our wine under the same *appellation*!' Heartfelt words, which met an enthusiastic response. But a name had to be found for the new *appellation* which would not revive old local jealousies. 'Thorins', which designated the wines of Romanèche, was just as unthinkable as 'Chénas'. What to do?

At this point, somebody – unknown to history – looked over at the hilltop crowned by its ancient windmill, a witness to at least three hundred grape harvests. 'How about calling it "Moulin-à-Vent"?' he suggested. And thus the first growth of the Beaujolais was born and subsequently authenticated by a series of judgements and rulings. Moulin-à-Vent arrived ten years before the AOCs; it was not until the decree of July 30, 1935 that *appellations d'origine* finally became *controlées*. At the same time a body was created to define, protect and regulate the AOCs – the *Comité National*, which later became the *Institut National des Appellations d'Origine des Vins et Eaux-de-vie* (INAO).

The conditions of production imposed by the 1935 decree eliminated a good number of *appellations* created by the earlier legislation. The idea of regulation also disgusted many wine-growers

VENDANGES EN BEAUJOLAIS

Collection LAMARSALLE, Villefranche

LES VENDANGES. — Les Porteurs.

65

66

and wine-merchants, who considered the *quid pro quo* of promotional advantage to be most uncertain.

In the Beaujolais, the opposite proved to be the case. The region saw itself well protected by the new legislation. Of course, the wine-growers had to submit to constraints as part of the bargain, but these were readily accepted and everyone set to work. Thus the Beaujolais was the first wine-producing region in France to be fully demarcated.

The only real problem was raised by the stubborn little commune of Chénas which still held out for its own *appellation*, with a production of eight hundred casks of wine. It was too late to join Moulin-à-Vent, whose boundaries had already been firmly fixed by a series of irrevocable judgements. Yet Chénas could hardly be struck off the map . . . so finally it was decided that the commune should be enlarged by a section of territory belonging to La Chapelle-du-Guinchay.

The last piece of the puzzle had finally fallen into place, and now the gradual conquest of the world market could begin in earnest.

BRIEF HISTORIES

'A product which pleases is already half sold.' . . . but only half. Victor Peyret, a wine-merchant with a small business at Juliénas, well knew this. Peyret was a great friend of the cartoonist, Henri Monnier, whom he often visited at the offices of the satirical newspaper, *Canard Enchaîné*, in Paris (well provided, of course, with bottles of his wine). In due course, this friendship led to others with the song-writers, *chansonniers*, of Montmartre, who in turn began to include allusions to Juliénas in their plays and cabaret revues. Victor Peyret had unwittingly discovered the virtues of advertising . . . a little like M Jourdain discovered prose. But Peyret's most heroic feat of arms was his purchase of the Hôtel du Beaujolais at Juliénas. The owner, who was exceedingly stingy, thought Juliénas wine over-priced and served a horrible rotgut bought cheap at the local grocery store. One evening, Victor Peyret, with a crowd of well-

disposed cronies, took the publican violently to task.

'Aren't you ashamed to serve such filthy stuff in Juliénas? If you can't run a proper bistro, you should sell up and join the church!'

'Well, if you're so clever, you can buy it yourself.'

'By God, so I will!'

And Victor Peyret signed yet another cheque . . . which he tried to get back the following day, when he had cooled off. But the publican, delighted with his windfall, didn't want to know. 'What's agreed is agreed', he said.

In the Beaujolais a man's word is his bond; at that time, agreements were still sealed by the slapping of palms, like at the cattle market of Saint-Christophe-en Brionnais. So Victor Peyret found himself the owner of the Hôtel du Beaujolais at Juliénas, where he installed his associate Gaby Ferraton. In time, the cooking of the Beaujolais was enriched by a new recipe for *coq au vin* invented here, and the establishment was renamed the Coq au Vin.

'SAINTE MARGUERITE DU BEAUJOLAIS'

The recognition of communal *appellations* by the 1935 decree gave rise to a certain chauvinism. Like Juliénas with Victor Peyret, each different *cru* organized its own propaganda through wine-merchants who urged their clients to buy such-and-such an *appellation*.

But at Fleurie, the Beaujolais had an able wine-growing advocate in the person of Marguerite Chabert, for whom the wine of her commune had attained an almost religious importance.

Marguerite Chabert swore to her dying father that she would direct the fortunes of the cooperative cellar at Fleurie for the greater good of all. She succeeded him as president and became the first woman head of a wine cooperative in France. So began a lifelong espousal of the cause of Fleurie.

This lady, with her broad hat and her refusal to turn down a glass of Beaujolais, provided it contained

SCÈNES CHAMPÊTRES
Le vieux Pressoir.

Fleurie, soon became a familiar figure in the region; everywhere she went she was accompanied by her bottles. With her straightforward manner, Marguerite Chabert has conferred on equal terms with the highest authorities. She has had only one inveterate enemy: the wine of the Midi, whose guiding powers refused to accept a woman's interference in their industry. The Beaujolais, nonetheless, owes her a debt of gratitude; she wears her heart on her sleeve and she is loyal to her friends, good-humoured, with a fiendish talent for quick repartee. Marguerite Chabert liked nothing better than a good meal at her house with somebody she considered worthy of appreciating a good bottle of wine. One day, after many months of entreaties, I accepted an invitation to lunch with her in one of the great restaurants of Paris, where she seemed to be far better known than the film stars seated around us.

The moment came to choose the wines. It was the end of the new wine season and Marguerite Chabert opted for a Beaujolais-Villages, with the comment that 'one would try to please all tastes'. When the cheese arrived, she said (with a broad smile): 'Now we need a really good wine. What do you suggest?' 'Mademoiselle', I replied, 'anything but Fleurie would be out of the question.'

She would never have expected any other answer; at the very name of Fleurie, her face lit up. But not for long, for the waiter came back, covered in confusion, to announce that there was no more Fleurie.

Marguerite went pale. Then she became upset and her hat began to tremble with the force of her indignation.

'Call the manager!'

The manager was an old friend and he was profoundly apologetic. Marguerite rebuked him kindly, and assured him she would see to it personally that he was sent an ample supply of bottles when she got home.

'Right, we shall have to do without our Fleurie for today. What shall we have?'

'Perhaps we could try the Juliénas.'

'Good idea. Waiter! give us a Juliénas, but only a half-bottle, please.'

Marguerite Chabert is indeed a great lady of the Beaujolais.

HOSPITALITY IN THE BEAUJOLAIS

The unification of Beaujolais wine-growers was brought about by a simple government decision, not by any law or decree. The state fixed prices for the 1944 harvest without consulting the growers' representatives. With the Nazi troops barely out of the area, it looked as if the Beaujolais might rebel against the government of the Liberation.

The local unions rose as one man. Not to build barricades, but to create a single association which was called the *Union Viticole du Beaujolais*. The

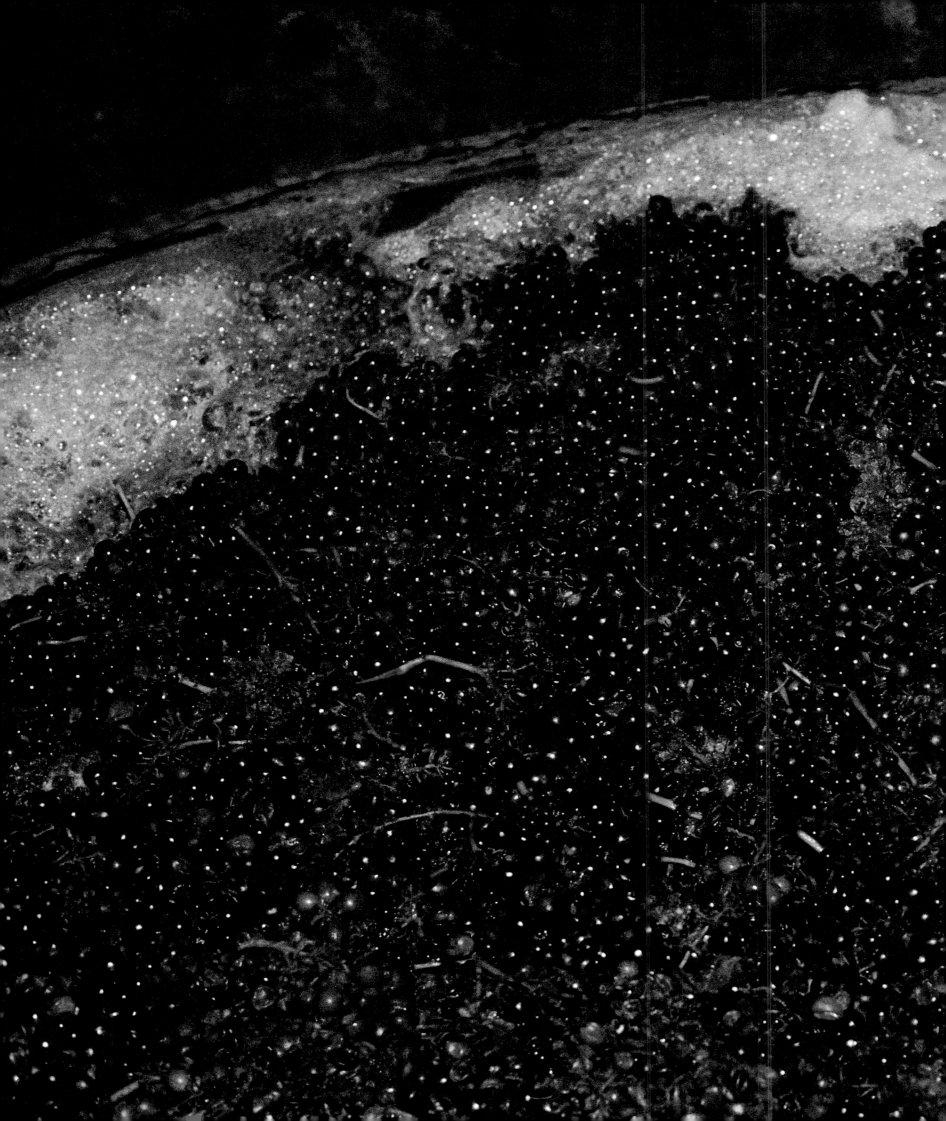

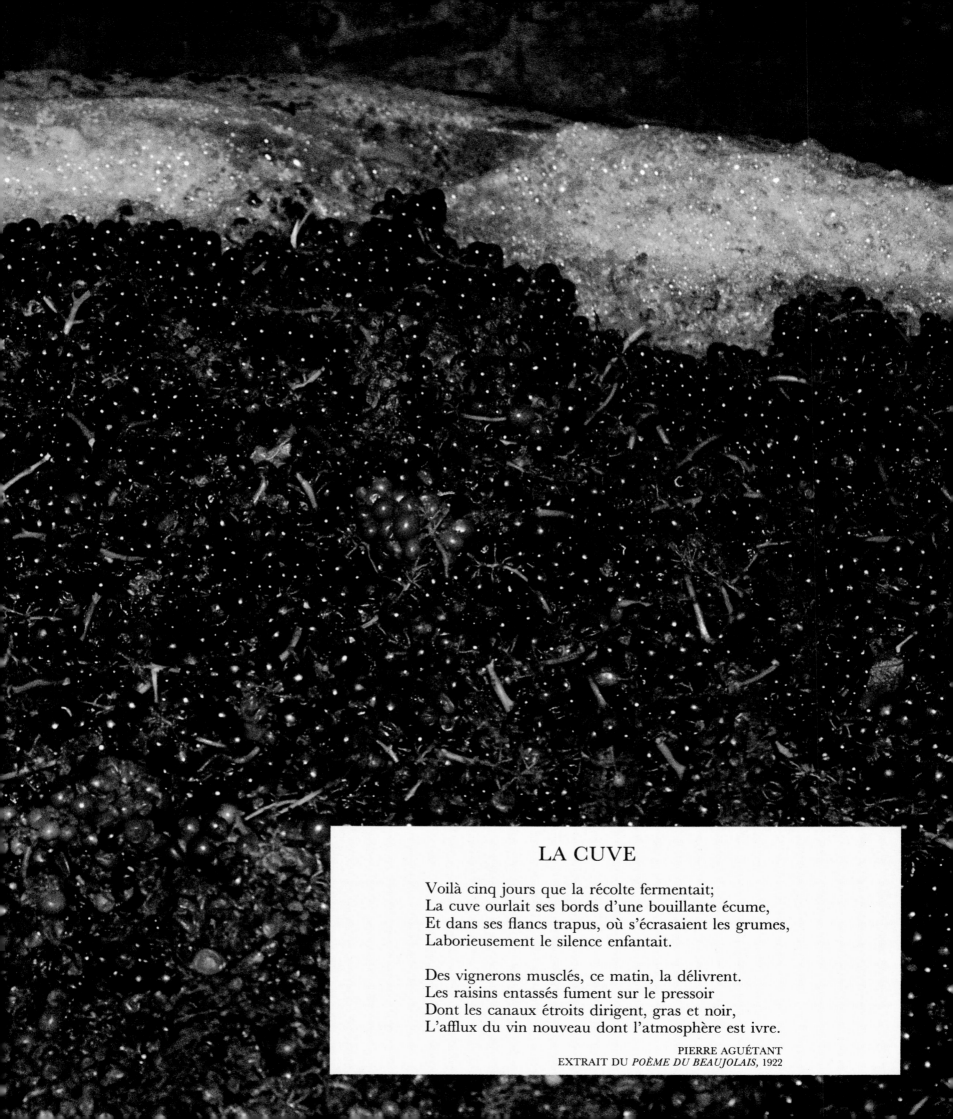

LA CUVE

Voilà cinq jours que la récolte fermentait;
La cuve ourlait ses bords d'une bouillante écume,
Et dans ses flancs trapus, où s'écrasaient les grumes,
Laborieusement le silence enfantait.

Des vignerons musclés, ce matin, la délivrent.
Les raisins entassés fument sur le pressoir
Dont les canaux étroits dirigent, gras et noir,
L'afflux du vin nouveau dont l'atmosphère est ivre.

PIERRE AGUÉTANT
EXTRAIT DU *POÈME DU BEAUJOLAIS,* 1922

DOMAINE BOUILLARD — 750 ML

Chiroubles

APPELLATION CHIROUBLES CONTRÔLÉE

Mise en bouteille au Domaine

René BOUILLARD, Viticulteur à CHIROUBLES (Rhône)

PRODUIT DE FRANCE

PRODUIT DE FRANCE

Côte de Brouilly

APPELLATION CONTRÔLÉE

DOMAINE DU PETIT PRESSOIR

Mis en bouteille par
Louis TÊTE à Saint-Didier-sur-Beaujeu (Rhône)

75 cl

Fleurie
"Grille Midi"

Appellation Fleurie Contrôlée

1982

MIS EN BOUTEILLE A ROMANÈCHE-THORINS
PAR LE SAVOUR CLUB, NÉGOCIANT A LANCIÉ (RHÔNE)

PRODUCE OF FRANCE

Savour Club

75 cl

Itinerant still

Beaujolais wine-growers had been the first to adopt the constraints imposed by the AOC system; they had even submitted themselves to voluntary regulations; but they still wished to be their own masters. France had been liberated, and they saw no reason to accept another form of slavery. . . .

This was the prevailing view among the wine-growers when they decided to bring together Beaujolais, Beaujolais-Villages and the *crus* under a single umbrella. Three men took command of a new association: Jean Laborde, the Beaujolais leader, a quiet man who later represented the constituency in the Chamber of Deputies; Jean Petit, the 'bulldozer' of Beaujolais-Villages; and Claude Geoffray, the jovial representative of the *grands crus*. By a curious twist of destiny, all three later died within months of each other. They were succeeded by one of their original team, Louis Bréchard, universally known as Papa Bréchard.

The Beaujolais wine-grower has always had a strong sense of hospitality. He is never happier than when showing a visitor round his cellar and offering him his wines to taste. One year, at his Château Thivin domain, Claude Geoffray sacrificed no less then seventeen casks of Brouilly to these tastings by visitors.

Claude Geoffray fully intended that the fame of Beaujolais should spread outside the Lyonnais, to Paris and beyond. The battle should be fought on behalf of the entire region, not on behalf of any particular *cru*. An unexpected social development, the mass use of the motorcar (particularly at peak holiday periods), added urgency to the matter.

Just after the war, there was no *autoroute* as yet, but on the RN6, known as the *Route du Soleil*, the traffic increased inexorably from year to year. Claude Geoffray contemplated the uninterrupted stream of vehicles and realized that if some of them could be induced to stop in the region they would be the source of fantastic publicity. Jean Laborde and Jean Petit reached the same conclusion. At a general meeting of the Wine Producing Union, *Union Viticole*, on

Grape-treading. (Painting on wood, private collection)

May 2, 1949, the three men described their idea for a typical Beaujolais house built of fine yellow stone, to be built beside the main road. The house would be sufficiently comfortable for visitors to stay and taste the whole range of local *appellations* at their leisure.

By the end of the year, the site had been chosen and plans drawn up by a Paris architect. The following spring, Claude Geoffray was in a state of high anticipation: a 'sales and advertising cooperative' had been created, with a capital of 120,000 francs, divided into thirty parts. By unanimous agreement, the cooperative was called La Maison des Beaujolais. One detail remained to be settled – ten million '1950' francs had to be found to finance the operation.

Fortune favours the brave, and Claude Geoffray launched the idea of a mass subscription: 10,000 shares at 1000 francs each. The 'impossible task' of selling these was entrusted to Jean Ravet, who worked for the Union Viticole. For over a year, the Union's little Simca zigzagged to and fro across the vineyards, often none too steadily, as the unfortunate Jean Ravet often found himself swallowing as many glasses of wine as he sold shares. But finally the miracle was accomplished; on March 30, 1952, the president of the *Conseil des Ministres*, Antoine Pinay, inaugurated the Maison des Beaujolais, in which nearly every wine-grower in the region had a stake.

Nowhere else in France has there been so remarkable a display of solidarity. But the road is long between the birth of a project and its accomplishment. The Maison des Beaujolais opened a fresh avenue of publicity. Villié-Morgon, led by its mayor and cooperative president, was soon committed to the creation of the first tasting-cellar in the area, which became the departure point for a long chain of bacchic staging posts.

Beaujolais also made some appearances at the Paris fairs and agricultural shows. The young wines were still in their infancy, but they were already beginning to look beyond France's borders. The Union Viticole began to draw closer to the mainstream of the wine trade. There was even talk of 'interprofessional' cooperation.

The year of 1959 precipitated matters. That year the government struck another blow by imposing a series of supplementary taxes. On top of this, it launched a campaign for the suppression of alcohol, which rapidly became an anti-wine crusade. The Beaujolais region was deeply offended and ceased to participate in official functions. This situation led to a *rapprochement* between wine-growers and wine-merchants, who, on September 25, 1959 created the *Union Interprofessionelle des Vins du Beaujolais*, with Antoine Chavand, a wise and diplomatic wine-grower, as its first president. To put the seal on this union, the new association decided to have its presidency alternate each year between wine-merchant and wine-grower. This was another arrangement that made the Beaujolais unique in all of France. Interprofessionalism has since followed the path mapped out by Victor Peyret, Claude Geoffray, Jean Laborde, Jean Petit and Marguerite Chabert, and it has built an

atmosphere of good-will throughout the Beaujolais. This atmosphere is the key to the region's success.

While the wine-growers were protesting against the new government measures, the Beaujolais had sent a small plump gentleman to represent it in the National Assembly. Louis Bréchard, a militant in the professional unions of some ten years' standing, had not yet acquired the title of *Papa*, but he was beginning to be known for his plain-speaking and occasional outbursts of temper. Bréchard had no taste for politics and finally came back to live among his own people. He travelled around the world to promote Beaujolais and was largely responsible for the conquest of the international market which was the goal of the interprofessional union.

Louis Bréchard was also an ardent defender of the wine-growers, and nicknamed the 'Lion of the Valley' by them. His battles against the administration have become legendary. Here is one story which he related himself:

One day, we had to conduct a series of very painstaking tastings, and the tax inspector was so ignorant of the way in which we made the wine that he wrote in his report: 'The wine-growers use no fuel to head their storehouses, but are content to plug the holes with old blankets'.

LES DIX COMMANDEMENTS
A L'USAGE DES BEAUJOLAISES

I

De bonne frigousse feras
A ton conjoint journellement.

II

Du beaujolais, le verseras
Aux amis pour contentement.

III

En pêche, aux boules enverras
Ton mari sans ressentiment.

IV

Chaque lundi tu te rendras
Au grand marché, plein d'agrément.

V

De cancanages, t'abstiendras
Et de ragots pareillement.

VI

De francs mamis enfanteras
Autant artets que leurs parents.

VII

Fricasse et bugnes te cuiras
Et matefaims, dévotement.

VIII

Le minois souriant, t'auras
Dans les embiernes mêmement.

IX

Ton époux ne gongonneras
Que s'il a bu tout son argent.

X

Et le même, te garderas
Sans le changer... de son vivant.

JULES PETITJEAN
EXTRAIT DE L'*ALMANACH DU BEAUJOLAIS*, 1956

Les **VENDANGES** — Repas des Vendangeurs

LÉMONON-DUCOTÉ ÉDIT MACON

Vermorel

SOCIÉTÉ ANONYME AU CAPITAL DE 8.000.000 DE FRANCS

REGISTRE DU COMMERCE VILLEFRANCHE S/S 145

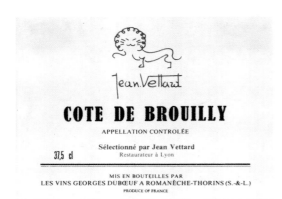

Then, after a pause, Papa Bréchard would slyly add: 'He wrote "old blankets" because if he'd mentioned new ones, he'd have had to calculate their depreciation . . .'

LA FÊTE

The Beaujolais wine-growers might agree with Montesquieu, when he says: 'I am in love with friendship.' The wine-grower exports friendship in his bottles; it is rooted in his work, in his vineyard and in the hearts of everyone who lives around him. Friendship is at the core of all the fêtes that take place in the Beaujolais.

The most famous of these is doubtless the *Fête des Conscrits de Villefranche*, held in the administrative capital of the Beaujolais ever since that day in 1850, when two jolly fellows went to the drawing of lots for conscription dressed in opera hats and evening dress. Each year, the young men born between the same dates in a decade parade down the main street of the town. On this occasion the conscripts always show a fine spirit of solidarity, with the wealthier boys taking charge of the poorer ones. This Villefranche custom has overflowed into the surrounding villages of the Beaujolais (though without its originally misogynous character). The *Fête des Conscrits* is the

occasion for a gathering of all generations and families in the village, with singing, dancing and a huge banquet.

In the view of Brillat-Savarin, the destinies of nations depend on the way they eat. In this sense the Beaujolais nation, as we have seen, can boast of its golden destiny. And there are no meetings between folks, no good times, without abundant meals . . . these take place at wine contests, agricultural shows, and on Saint-Vincent's Day, when the wine-growers of most communes still celebrate their patron saint. Nowadays, professional meetings have often replaced the cult of Saint-Vincent in gentlemen's houses, but the meals are still as copious and the wine flows as freely as ever. People also take time to eat especially well on the night before the first of May, when, in a revival of the ancient pagan tradition, young people go from house to house toasting the arrival of the first month without an 'R' in it. Voltaire maintained that since pigs were made to be eaten, men should consume pork all year round. In the Beaujolais, this advice is followed to the letter and a pig-killing is always an excuse for a real party. In the old days, every wine-grower raised his own pig. Today, he relies on the pork butcher, but the *Saint-Cochon* is still ritually observed, with much excitement in the house and a marvellous *fricassée de boudins* shared with the neighbours.

The people of the Beaujolais may be proud and harsh in their working habits, but their greatest joy is to entertain and adopt visitors. Each village has its own fête, but every five years there is a general mobilization for the great *Fêtes du Beaujolais*, which attracts many thousands of visitors from all over the world.

The 'Beaujolais success story' is talked about everywhere. The key to it is perfectly simple, and Gabriel Chevallier, the author of *Clochemerle*, has summed it up to perfection:

'The people of this place see to it that love, harmony and joy prevail over everything, because Beaujolais is a damn good wine which never does any harm. The more you drink of it,

the more delightful you find your wife, the more loyal your friends, the rosier your future and the more bearable mankind. All the evil in the world can be traced to a single fact: that there is only one Beaujolais on the face of the planet. This is the country of the elect and they all have good wine-lover's faces and spirited manners. They offer their hearts in the palms of one hand . . . the hand, that is, that does not hold a glass.'

Pipette *and* tastevin: *two instruments of Beaujolais hospitality*

APPELLATIONS OF THE BEAUJOLAIS

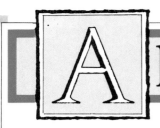

Charles QUITTANSON

As the proverb goes, *dura lex sed lex*; the law is harsh, but it's the law. Beaujolais submits to the law and is in turn submitted to careful government controls.

The Beaujolais viticultural region produces practically nothing but wines entitled to the AOC label. But what exactly is an *appellation d'origine*?

This ancient idea, which is fundamental in French law, is defined as follows by the law of July 6, 1966, which complements the modified organic law of May 6, 1919, relative to the protection of *appellations d'origine*:

'Shall constitute an *appellation d'origine*, the denomination of a country, area or locality which serves to describe a product originating there and whose quality or characteristics are due to geographic surroundings, including both natural and human factors.'

Hence an *appellation d'origine* qualifies products of quality, whose type and originality are bound to geography (the soil for example), and which owe their specific characteristics to 'natural factors' (such as ground, exposition, altitude, hygrometry, winds, vine varieties, and 'human factors' (vine cultivation, pruning, methods of harvesting and vinification, distillation processes, wine storage methods).

The *appellation controlée* dates from the decree of July 30, 1035, which also created the INAO, a body whose function is to review the rules governing the production of fine wines and brandies, notably on the basis of 'local, honest and consistent' practices. Hence the *appellation controlée* is an evolved form of *appellation d'origine*.

APPELLATIONS D'ORIGINE CONTROLÉE *IN THE BEAUJOLAIS*

There are eleven AOCs in the Beaujolais:

– Regional *appellations*: Beaujolais (and Beaujolais Supérieur), Beaujolais-Villages (and Beaujolais followed by the name of one of the classified communes).
– *Cru appellations* (north to south): Saint-Amour (Saône-et-Loire), Juliénas, Chénas, Moulin-à-Vent, Fleurie, Chiroubles, Morgon, Côte-de-Brouilly, Brouilly (Rhône).
Refer to the table overleaf for the prescribed status of each.

The *appellation* Beaujolais Supérieur can be claimed by the entire area covered by the Beaujolais *appellation*. The *appellation* Beaujolais, followed by the name of a commune, may only be

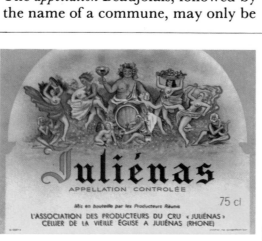

obtained by a certain number of restrictively designated communes. These are the following:
Rhône: Juliénas, Jullié, Emeringes, Chénas, Fleurie, Chiroubles, Lancié, Villié-Morgon, Lantigné, Beaujeu, Régnié, Durette, Cercié, Quincié, Saint-Lager, Odenas, Charentay, Saint-Etienne-La-Varenne, Vaux, Le Perréon, Saint-Etienne-des-Ouillières, Blacé, Arbuissonnas, Salles, Saint-Julien, Montmelas, Rivolet, Denicé, Les Ardillats, Marchampt, Vauxrenard.
Saône-et-Loire: Leynes, Saint-Armour-Bellevue, La Chapelle-de-Guinchay, Romanèche-Thorins, Pruzilly, Chanes, Saint-Vérand, Saint-Symphorien-d'Ancelles.

These wines can also claim the *appellation* Beaujolais-Villages. The decree of May 6, 1946 opened the right to the *appellation* Bourgogne to wines already possessing a *cru appellation*. In the canton of La Chapelle-de-Guinchay, the principle adopted is the separation of areas giving the right either to the AOC Beaujolais or the AOC Mâcon. The southern boundary of the Mâcon area is confused with the southern boundary of the Saint-Veran area (specifically, two streams, the Arlois and the Préty, are the limits). Hence the communes of Romanèche, La Chapelle, Saint-Symphorien, Saint-Amour and Pruzilly are to be excluded from Mâcon. The assorted red and rosé wines of one of the Beaujolais, Beaujolais Supérieur or Beaujolais-Villages *appellations* may be considered as young wines, *vins de primeur*, and sold for immediate consumption after November 18 of the year of harvest, provided they fulfil the following conditions:
● Volatile acidity below 0.60 g/litre (in H_2SO_4);
● Maximum of 2 g/litre of residual sugar content for red and rosé wines;
● Prior tasting conducted under the aegis of the INAO.

The regulations do not, however, stipulate any time limit for the selling

Le Beaujolais

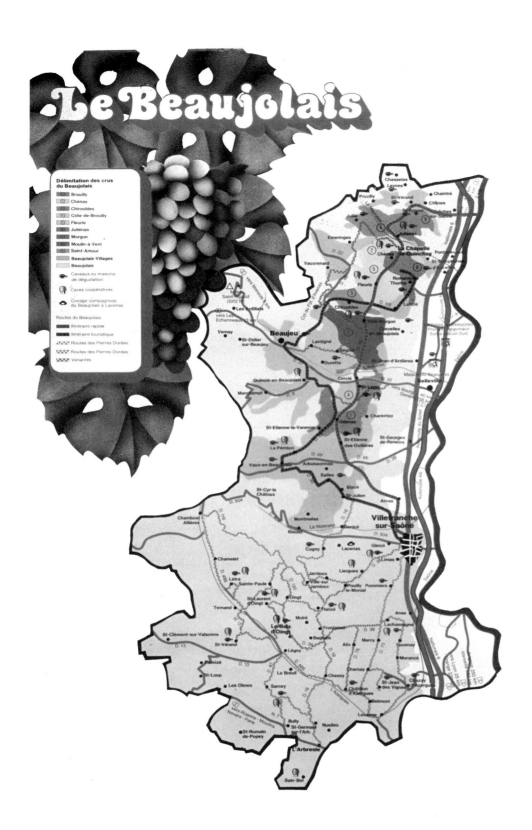

Délimitation des crus du Beaujolais

- Brouilly
- Chénas
- Chiroubles
- Côte-de-Brouilly
- Fleurie
- Juliénas
- Morgon
- Moulin-à-Vent
- Saint-Amour
- Beaujolais-Villages
- Beaujolais
- Caveaux ou maisons de dégustation
- Caves coopératives
- Cuvage compagnons du Beaujolais à Lacenas

Routes du Beaujolais

- Itinéraire rapide
- Itinéraire touristique
- Routes des Pierres Dorées
- Routes des Pierres Dorées
- Variantes

of *vins de primeur*. They should, however, be taken off the market, at the very latest, by the end of the spring following the harvest. This is because their freshness is lost as soon as the warm weather returns.

BEAUJOLAIS VINIFICATION

The following information is taken from an excellent brochure published by the INAO.

Beaujolais vinification may be defined as a vinification of whole grapes which are allowed to macerate for three to seven days. The Beaujolais is the only viticultural region in the world which has preserved this ancestral method, which is often referred to as 'carbonic semi-maceration'. 'Beaujolais vinification' would be more appropriate to describe the superimposition of two phenomena deriving from classic red, *en rouge*, vinification and carbonic maceration. The difference is as follows:

● In a red-pressed vinification, *vinification en rouge foulée*, the wine undergoes a single liquid phase of fermentation. In this form of fermentation, yeasts produce enzymes, causing a series of reactions which ultimately convert sugar into alcohol and secondary substances.

● In a carbonic maceration process, whole grapes are fed into a closed vat which has previously been saturated with carbon dioxide. Thereafter, the wine goes through two parallel phases the liquid phase (the less extensive), consisting of fermenting must derived from grapes crushed during transfer to the vat or by the weight of other grapes; and the solid phase, consisting of the fermentation inside each undamaged grape.

FRANKREICH   1983

Beaujolais

VIN NOUVEAU

Appellation Beaujolais Contrôlée

Ce Beaujolais a été mis en bouteille dès sa naissance pour les amateurs de vins primeurs. Dégustez ce vin dès que possible, **et servez-le frais** pour en savourer tout le fruit.

Mis en bouteille dans la région de production par

1 l

PASQUIER-DESVIGNES
au Marquisat depuis 1420, Négociants Eleveurs à St Lager, Rhône France

PRODUCE OF FRANCE

Beaujolais

APPELLATION CONTRÔLÉE

Ets T. DAVID & L. FOILLARD
NÉGOCIANTS A SAINT-GEORGES-DE-RENEINS (RHONE)

The liquid phase is classic alcoholic fermentation brought about by yeasts; but in the solid phase, a kind of intra-cellular reaction takes place. The cells inside the grape need energy to stay alive. When they have access to air, they acquire this energy by breathing. If the grape is plunged into an airless atmosphere in which oxygen is replaced by carbon dioxide, for a short while it continues to breathe the residual oxygen contained between its tissue cells. When this oxygen has been used up, the metabolism of the grape changes and it seeks to draw life energy from the intra-cellular fermentation of its reserves.

The result is a progressive exhaustion of these reserves and the subsequent death of the grape's cells, which are asphyxiated by residues,

Heavyweight tasting. From left to right: Paul Bocuse, Jean de Saint-Charles, Georges Duboeuf, Pierre Troisgros

notably alcohol. This intra-cellular fermentation operates in the absence of micro-organisms (yeast or bacteria). At the end of the intra-cellular process the consistency of the skins alters and they expel all their elements into the pulp. Up to two per cent of alcohol may form in the grape and malic acid may break down in a proportion of thirty to forty per cent, without formation of lactic acid.

Beaujolais vinification also has its liquid and solid phases. The liquid part undergoes classic alcoholic fermentation, and represents ten to twenty per cent of the total volume of material placed in the vat and twenty-five to fifty per cent of what is subsequently taken from it. The solid part is progressively saturated with carbon dioxide by the juice fermenting at the bottom of the vat. Thus there is a more or less advanced intra-cellular fermentation, according to the length of time the wine is left in the vat; but this fermentation never reaches its final stage.

THE WINES OF THE BEAUJOLAIS – AN OUTLINE

We shall confine ourselves here to red wines, since whites and rosés, although distinctive, are still rare in the region.

Beaujolais

The wine known as Beaujolais is mainly produced to the south and west of Villefranche, in the *arrondissement* of Beaujolais. Here the soil is limestone-clay, with occasional sandy patches.

Beaujolais pure and simple is the café wine, *vin de comptoir*, which used to be drunk from heavy forty-five-centilitre bottles, *pots*. It is a vigorous proletarian wine which goes down the throat and out again after the most perfunctory passage through the kidneys. The dominant smells are flowery and fruity; vegetable, rather than animal as in the Pinot Noir wines of the Côte-d'Or. Beaujolais is a wine that must be drunk young, to preserve its freshness and youthful innocence.

CHÂTEAU DE LA GRANDE GRANGE

BEAUJOLAIS-VILLAGES

APPELLATION BEAUJOLAIS-VILLAGES CONTRÔLÉE

MIS EN BOUTEILLES AU CHÂTEAU PAR

GEORGES DUBŒUF À 71720 ROMANÈCHE-THORINS, FRANCE

PRODUCE OF FRANCE

37,5 cl

beaujolais 1970

appellation contrôlée

spécialement choisi pour vous par

la grande cuisine française

mis en bouteilles par

georges dubœuf à romanèche-thorins - 71

Les Sommeliers Parisiens à la Grange.

86

BEAUJOLAIS-VILLAGES
APPELLATION CONTROLÉE
SÉLECTIONNÉ ET MIS EN BOUTEILLES EN EXCLUSIVITÉ
POUR FAG DISTRIBUTION PAR QUINSON et FILS

LA VIEILLE CUVE DU PÈRE PALLANCHER

69820 FLEURIE RHONE FRANCE
PRODUCE OF FRANCE
75 cl

Côte de Brouilly
Appellation Contrôlée
75 cl

QUINSON FILS
NÉGOCIANT-ÉLEVEUR A FLEURIE (RHONE) - FRANCE
PRODUCE OF FRANCE

– Régnié – Le 10 Août 1926

Beaujolais-Villages

Beaujolais-Villages comes from granitic soils, like the region's *crus*. The vine variety is the clear-juiced black Gamay, as elsewhere. The red-juiced black Gamay is forbidden in the area, since it would add an element of vulgarity and an unwelcome dark colour to the wine. Beaujolais-Villages is generally full, but sufficiently robust to keep in bottles for one or two years. It has a more distinctive smell than simple Beaujolais, and has a larger taste due to its firm body.

The Nine *Crus*

The nine *crus* of the Beaujolais are great rivals. Which of them is the best? Like the poet, we say: 'One may as well try to choose between nine pretty girls. Better make love to all of them!'

Saint-Amour

The northernmost *cru* of the Beaujolais, popularized by Louis Dailly.
– Area: 275 hectares. Average production: 13,000 hectolitres.
– Full-blooded wine, known for lightness and voluptuousness rather than finesse. Ages well, but only for a relatively short period.
– Dominant odour: peach, apricot, peony.

Juliénas

This wine was rediscovered by the *Canard Enchaîné* fifty years ago. There is a proverb which maintains 'One should never trust a man who drinks his Juliénas in one swallow'.
– The soil of Juliénas, in the canton of Beaujeu, is generally loamy.
– Area: 560 hectares. Average production: 25,000 hectolitres.
– Solid, firm, nervy at the end of the season. Ages well, though the Juliénas of Jullié and Emeringes tends to be more precocious.
– Dominant aromas: red fruits like cherry, raspberry, blood-peach.

Chénas

The soil is granitic, manganese-rich and salmon-pink in colour. Part of the commune of Chénas is included in

the Moulin-à-Vent area.
– Area: 270 hectares. Average
production: 12,000 hectolitres.
– More aroma than Juliénas. Spicy,
generous, warm and firm, though
refined. The wine has a tender
quality which becomes more
pronounced on the La Chapelle-de-
Guinchay side.
– Dominant aroma: peony.

Moulin-à-Vent

The vineyard surrounds the famous
windmill which dominates the
landscape. (There is no village of
Moulin-à-Vent.) The two communes
which produce Moulin-à-Vent are
Chénas and Romanèche-Thorins, a
straggling village in which the first
exhibition of Beaujolais Nouveau is
held annually (known as the *Fête
Raclet*). The soil is a manganese-
bearing, disintegrated granite (known
as *gore*).
– Area: 780 hectares; average
production: 35,000 hectolitres.
– A serious and vital (*racé*) wine,
which ages very well; reminiscent of
the great Côte-d'Or Burgundies.
Robust and generous, strong colour.
– Dominant aromas: violets and
(especially) iris.

Fleurie

The excellent reputation of this *cru*
has been carefully nourished by
Marguerite Chabert, president of the
Fleurie Cooperative and a great
character in the annals of the
Beaujolais.
– Area: 780 hectares. Average
production: 40,000 hectolitres.
– A lady's wine, refined and silky.
Fleurie is also light in body; but is not
for keeping too long.
– Dominant aromas: amber, iris,
above all violets.

Chiroubles

The village of Chiroubles, nestling in its bowl of granitic soil, is famous for the exploit of one of its people, Victor Pulliat, who, in 1888, perfected the technique of grafting on to American rootstock, thereby saving the vines of France. Chiroubles has its own natural terrace, from which the entire Beaujolais may be seen; and its *cru* is the youngest of the region's wines.
– Area: 345 hectares. Average production: 13,000 hectolitres.
– A full-bodied, fruity, distinctive and tender wine.
– Dominant aromas: violets, iris, mignonette.

Morgon

The vines of this *cru* surround the commune of Villié-Morgon. The soils here are unusual, being composed of broken pyritic shale. This is known as disintegrated rock, *roche pourrie*.
– Area: 1000 hectares. Average production: 50,000 hectolitres.
– The wine of Morgon is substantial and generous, with a dark garnet-red colour and a characteristic taste. It ages well.
– Dominant aromas: kirsch, cherry, quince.

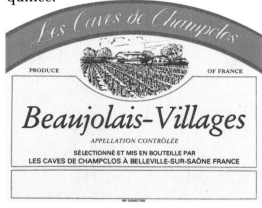

Tasse *belonging to Léon Foillard, founder of the* Compagnons du Beaujolais

Côte-de-Brouilly

The vineyards of Côte-de-Brouilly stand on the slopes of Mont Brouilly (300 metres), which dominates the region. The soil contains volcanic sand.
– Area: 310 hectares. Average production: 9000 hectolitres.
– A garnet-red wine, substantial, full flavoured, warm and very fruity. Ages well, although its fruitiness tends to fade with time and is replaced by other properties.

Brouilly

The wines of the Brouilly *appellation* grow along the foothills of the Côte de Brouilly, on porphyritic soil. The reputation of this *cru* rests largely on the work of Claude Geoffray, one of the leaders of the movement to establish *appellations d'origine*.
– Area: 1125 hectares. Average production: 45,000 hectolitres.
– Wines to be drunk young; their effect is one of 'inner delight'. Fruity, flavour of fresh grapes.

Beaujolais Primeur

This wine is something apart; every year between one-third and a half of the harvest is drained off in the form of young wine. Beaujolais Primeur is the high-coloured, puppyish, stammering, yet delightful precursor of the maturer Beaujolais to come.

Beaujolais Nouveau sings a song of its own. Its colours are those of the harlequin; red, shining, clear as dawn, shimmering like a rainbow, flowing like spring water.

Beaujolais Nouveau has diabolical charm. It enraptures the drinker, despite its lightness. But, perhaps the last word should be left to René Fallet, who wrote in his famous novel:

. . . And the Beaujolais Nouveau arrived.

And from the North to the Midi, as on every 18th of November of every year, a springtime of little sky blue, red, orange and green posters flowered in the wineshops, announcing to gloomy passers-by that the infant Jesus of wines was born. And the gloomy passers-by brightened at the sight of these leaflets and a droplet of ruby fell into their grey lives, and clung like red confetti to their lips.

AOC	Production varieties			Minimum alcometric level before enrichment and after fermentation			Basic yield per hectare in production		This wine may also be given the *appellation*
	VR	Vr	VB	VR	Vr	VB	VR + Vr	VB	
For all AOCs	Authorised 15% maximum proportion of white vines in red or rosé wines			Degree acquired and potential					
Beaujolais	G, P	G, P	G, Pb, A	9 %	9 %	9,5 %	55 hl	55 hl	BGO
Beaujolais supérieur	»	»	»	10 %	10 %	10,5 %	55 hl	55 hl	Bjs, BGO
Beaujolais + nom commune d'origine	»	»	»	10 %	10 %	10,5 %	50 hl	55 hl	BS, Bjs, BGO
Beaujolais-Villages	»	»	»	10 %	10 %	10,5 %	50 hl	55 hl	BS, Bjs, BGO
Saint-Amour	G			10 %			48 hl		Bjs Or, BV, BS, Bjs, Bgne, BGO
Saint-Amour + nom climat d'origine	G			11 %			48 hl		Saint-Amour, Bjs Or, BV, BS, Bjs, Bgne, BGO
Juliénas	G			10 %			48 hl		Bjs Or, BV, BS, Bjs, Bgne, BGO
Juliénas + nom climat d'origine	G			11 %			48 hl		Juliénas, Bjs Or, BS, BV, Bjs, Bgne, BGO
Chénas	G			10 %			48 hl		Bjs Or, BV, BS, Bjs, Bgne, BGO
Chénas + nom climat d'origine	G			11 %			48 hl		Chénas, Bjs Or, BV, BS, Bjs, Bgne, BGO
Moulin-à-Vent	G			10 %			48 hl		Bjs Or, BV, BS, Bjs, Bgne, BGO
Moulin-à-Vent + nom climat d'origine	G			11 %			48 hl		Moulin-à-Vent, Bjs Or, BV, BS, Bjs, Bgne, BGO
Fleurie	G			10 %			48 hl		Bjs Or, BV, BS, Bjs, Bgne, BGO
Fleurie + nom climat d'origine	G			11 %			48 hl		Fleurie, Bjs Or, BV, BS, Bjs, Bgne, BGO
Chiroubles	G			10 %			48 hl		Bjs Or, BV, BS, Bjs, Bgne, BGO
Chiroubles + nom climat d'origine	G			11 %			48 hl		Chiroubles, Bjs Or, BV, BS, Bjs, Bgne, BGO
Morgon	G			10 %			48 hl		Bjs Or, BV, BS, Bjs, Bgne, BGO
Morgon + nom climat d'origine	G			11 %			48 hl		Morgon, Bjs Or, BV, BS, Bjs, Bgne, BGO
Côte-de-Brouilly	G, P			10,5 %			48 hl		Bjs Or, BV, BS, Bjs, Bgne, BGO, non en Brouilly
Côte-de-Brouilly + nom climat d'origine	G, P			11 %			48 hl		Côte-de-Brouilly, Bjs Or, BV, BS, Bjs, Bgne, BGO, non en Brouilly
Brouilly	G			10 %			48 hl		Bjs Or, BV, BS, Bjs, Bgne, BGO

Nom climat d'origine = Place of origin
Nom commune d'origine = Commune of origin

● **VR** = Vin Rouge; **Vr** = *Vin Rosé*: **VB**: *Vin Blanc*.
● **G** = Essential variety in red and rosé: clear-juiced Gamay.
● **P** = Authorized varieties: *Pinot Noir, Pinot Gris*.
● **C** = Essential variety for white wine: Chardonnay.
● **Pb** = Authorized varieties: *Pinot Blanc*.
● **A** = Aligoté.

BGO: Bourgogne Grand Ordinaire; **BS:** Beaujolais Supérieur; **BV** = Beaujolais-Villages; **Bgne:** Bourgogne; **Bjs** = Beaujolais; **Bjs Or** = Beaujolais, followed by commune of origin.
● Basic yield may be raised before attaining the limit allowed by the classification.

Pierre CARTIER

1981
Beaujolais

APPELLATION CONTRÔLÉE

Mis en bouteille par
FAYE NÉGOCIANT-ÉLEVEUR A F 71570   70 cl

SHIPPED BY WOODFORD BOURNE
PRODUCT OF FRANCE   FRENCH BOTTLED

GRAND VIN   BEAUJOLAIS   75 cl

BROUILLY

APPELLATION CONTRÔLÉE
MISE EN BOUTEILLES PAR LE VIGNERON

Félix CHAMPIER et Philippe Fils, viticulteurs, « Les Jacquets » ODENAS (Rhône). Tél. (74) 03.42.61

A Villefranche-sur-Saône, aux établissements Lachize et Reymuet, on vérifie le beaujolais qui sera livré dans les bistrots lyonnais.

DOMAINE DES BLEMONTS

RÉCOLTE 1974

CHENAS

APPELLATION CHENAS CONTRÔLÉE

73 cl

ROGER PELLOUX - Propriétaire Récoltant
LA CHAPELLE DE GUINCHAY (Saône-et-Loire) FRANCE

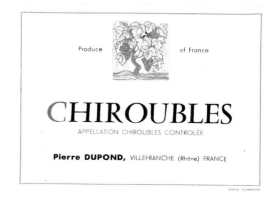

Produce   of France

CHIROUBLES

APPELLATION CHIROUBLES CONTRÔLÉE

Pierre DUPOND, VILLEFRANCHE (Rhône) FRANCE

INE *CRUS* OF CHARACTER

Gaston CHARLE

DIVERSITY IN UNITY

Just south of Mâcon, the N6 to Lyon skirts one of France's most beautiful vineyard regions: the Beaujolais.

Several million years ago, during the geological convulsions of the Hercynian era, the Massif Central threw up a series of small to medium-sized hills along its eastern fringes. The slopes of these hills are now wholly given over to the cultivation of the vine.

If by chance the passing motorist decides to turn off the N6, or the *autoroute* which runs parallel, to do a little exploring, he will discover the headwaters of the 'third river' so much revered by the people of the Lyonnais region. From the summit of Mont Saint-Rigaud (1012 metres), the eye takes in a vista of 20,000 hectares of vines, bathed in pure sunlight for most of the early spring; a quiet, modest landscape belying a long and eventful history.

Here and there, over a hundred sonorous church towers rise from this ocean of vines. Beyond them stretches the long silver ribbon of the tranquil river Saône, which marks the frontier between Beaujolais and Dombes. Finally, on the horizon, the huge mass of Mont Blanc dominates the high ridges of the distant Alps.

Every year, in these surroundings, the soil of the Beaujolais renders up 1,200,000 hectolitres of wine – 160 million bottles!

All the wines of the Beaujolais are made from a single grape variety: the clear-juiced black Gamay. The Gamay is thus the father of the eleven *appellations* of the Beaujolais and of several thousand *cuvées* of infinite diversity every year. But the Gamay was not always the dominant grape of the region.

Today, it is ranked third among all the varieties grown in France, with 50,000 hectares in cultivation (excluding its coloured variations). Philip the Strong's 1395 edict sought to stamp out the '*infame gamay*' altogether, stipulating that all Gamay vines in Burgundy should be uprooted.

Later, the aldermen of Mâcon congratulated themselves on the gift bestowed on them by nature of 'land full suited to producing the best wines for men's health, whilst the Beaujolais can only show wines that are greatly harmful to the human body, since the country thereabouts is only good for

Gamay vines, a breed of grape the use of which is forbidden in many places', especially in the county of Burgundy, because it was by nature 'greatly corrosive'.

Three centuries have passed; the Mâconnais has found its proper path, its own variety of vine, and its wine. As to the Gamay, which is the preferred vine for acid soils, it has given Beaujolais an unrivalled reputation as a carafe wine, just as it has spawned a whole range of *crus*, closely related but each with its own character.

But unity goes beyond the grape variety. Technology has developed a single type of vinification for the Beaujolais: the maceration of whole uncrushed grapes with their stalks.

It is at this stage that the influence of man becomes decisive. The lengthening or shortening of the maceration process influences the final constitution of the wine, more especially its degree of suppleness, which in turn affects its aptitude for early consumption or, conversely, the growth of its ageing potential, and thus decides whether it may be sold within a few months, or within a few years, according to the *appellation*.

Moreover, the *Primeur* wines which flood Paris and Lyon (on the third Thursday in November of each year) are no longer contained within the handful of communes which originally built their reputation. Time was when Percheron horses used to go down to the Loire, stopping by Les

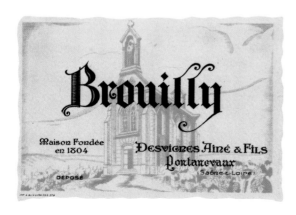

Echarmeaux to load the full casks of Beaujolais. The bungs of the casks would be pierced and a straw struck in the hole would allow the small belches of carbonic gas to bubble out of the young wine as it travelled down the road. *Autres temps, autres moeurs*. The unfermented wines of the old days gave way to the *Vin Primeur* which now flows from every corner of the Beaujolais, shaped as it is by the will of the wine-grower. The latter's art, coupled with an appropriate and generally shortened period of fermentation, compensates for the effects – and sometimes the excesses – of any given soil. The wine-grower also accelerates the post-fermentation stages in order to facilitate early bottling, whilst mobilizing the resources of modern oenology to stabilize his product as soon as possible.

The all-powerful client wants his wine to be faultless. It must be limpid, gas-free, reduced to essentials, and innocent of the least sediment. The client must be satisfied as far as possible without allowing mechanical or chemical processes to detract from the wine's originality. Its quality potential and its resources of scent must be preserved, for each Beaujolais possesses its own special perfume from the very first. The oenologist refers to this as 'aroma'; the wine-lover calls it 'fruitiness'.

FRUIT AND FLOWERS

The wines of the Beaujolais are essentially aromatic. The 'fruitiness' contributed by the ripe grape is a fragile and ephemeral quality. This fragility decides the choice of whole-grape vinification, which is the only

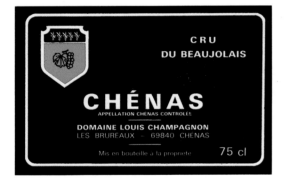

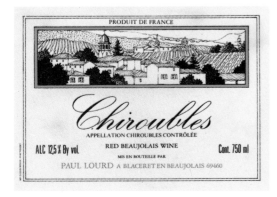

STANCES AU VIN BEAUJOLAIS

O beaujolais, pourquoi l'on t'aime
Tu le sauras assurément
En connaissant nos sentiments
Alors, tu le verras, toi-même,
O beaujolais, pourquoi l'on t'aime...

Tout d'abord, c'est notre œil qui t'aime
Pour ta couleur au teint vermeil
Semblable au rayon de soleil
Qui remplit le cœur tout plein d'ème.
C'est pour ta couleur que l'on t'aime...

Ensuite, c'est le nez qui t'aime
Pour ton parfum fin et discret
Qu'on dirait des fleurs d'un bouquet
Cueilli par le Per'Noé même
C'est pour ton parfum que l'on t'aime.

O beaujolais, pourquoi l'on t'aime,
C'est pour ton fruité savoureux
Qu'on dirait un Nectar des Dieux
Ou bien la Jouvence suprême
C'est pour tout cela que l'on t'aime...

CHANSON COMPOSÉE PAR JULES PETITJEAN
EXTRAIT DE L'*ALMANACH DU BEAUJOLAIS*, 1957

process by which the wine's primary aromatic components can be fixed. The revelation of this aroma is what gives new wine its great charm and its power to delight our tastebuds.

The complexity of aromatic substances, often only found in infinitesimal quantities in the wine, makes them difficult to assess in any qualitative way. Man's olfactive equipment, coupled with a certain amount of training of his sensory memory, is all he has to help him capture these subtleties and nuances. At this point we enter the enchanted garden of wine impressions based on the scents of flowers or fruit, rustic savours, or woodland smells. In the range of Beaujolais wines we are apt to come across the odours of lime-blossom, hawthorn, peach, peony, raspberry, apples, bergamot, cherry, rose, redcurrant, blackcurrant, banana, acid drops – and many others, both simple and complex. All these scents and smells are released by the circular movement of the wine in the glass; they blend and separate in an extraordinary symphony . . . an intricate dance of aromatic cells which sometimes allows one dominant feature to break through, reflecting the soil of the *cru*.

The identification of a *cru* by its dominant odours opens a number of perspectives to specialists in the initial phase of the life of the wine, before oxidation has modified the components of the aroma and turned them into a *bouquet*. Without laying down any hard-and-fast rules, a wine can be recognized through its (usually) dominant aroma. With Morgon, it is cherry; with Chiroubles, violets; Brouilly and Côte-de-Brouilly, the smell of fresh grapes, blackcurrants or redcurrants. Moulin-à-Vent and Chénas share a scent of faded roses; Juliénas is like peonies; Fleurie the iris; Saint-Amour the yellow peach; and Beaujolais and the young Beaujolais-Villages the odour of bananas.

SOIL AND CLIMATE

The vineyard soils of the Beaujolais derive from two geological formations, which meet at the level of Villefranche. These are:

– The crystalline massifs of the north, connecting the eastern edge of the Massif Central.
– The secondary formations of the south, which are made up of clay-limestone soils of sedimentary origin.

The soils derived from the ancient massifs are shallow, highly porous, poor and acid; rocky outcrops covered with a few centimetres of meagre soil. Each time this earth is swept down the hill by storms, men have tirelessly carried it up again. The parcels of ground are often surrounded by drystone walls, which

bear witness to the courage of the old land-reclaimers and their skill in the use of the crowbar. It is here, in the volcanic granite of these formations, that the Gamay vine yields its best results, in the form of Beaujolais-Villages and *Crus*.

The clay-limestone soil of the south contains stones tinged with yellow by iron oxides, turning golden when exposed to the sun. This is the *pierre dorée* which illuminates the south of the Beaujolais and its fine old houses. These colder, deeper, richer soils provide the basic Beaujolais wine, which was often called a bastard wine but now bears comparison with the very best.

The climate of the Beaujolais is generally temperate, though there are extremes of temperature. But since we are talking about vines, more importance should be attached to microclimatic conditions than to regional approximations. Firstly, the hills of the Beaujolais are sheltered by a screen of hills from the cold, wet winds that sweep up the Loire valley, often bringing stormy weather. Secondly, the vines grow on east-facing slopes which look out across the Saône basin. The Saône plays its part in regulating local temperatures, whilst the light that fills its broad plain favours the assimilation of chlorophyll in the ripening grapes. Lastly, the moderate altitude of the vineyards, combined with a gradient steep enough to allow satisfactory drainage, provides the right conditions for the cultivation of quality vines.

FAVOURABLE DEVELOPMENTS

The Beaujolais wine area was originally divided into two zones: Beaujolais and *appellations locales*. From the beginning, the legal arrangements carried the seeds for a third family, which is now well known under the name of Beaujolais-Villages. The Beaujolais production area, which covers 9,600 hectares, lies to the south and west of Villefranche, between the Nizerand and Azergues rivers in the Villefranche district, with a small abutment into five communes of the Lyon district. The *Pierres Dorées* road leads into the heart of the regional *appellation*, which is mostly on clay-limestone, with occasional strips of sandy and granitic soil. The erosion caused by rain adds to this mixture.

The wine-grower of the southern Beaujolais, who for centuries was half farmer, half wine-grower, did not always make the best use of his vines. His vinification methods left much to be desired and the wine often acquired an excessive and unpleasant taste from the earth. The receptacles he used, which were almost exclusively made of wood, tended to deteriorate; they were difficult to repair or replace, with barrel-makers becoming more and more rare.

The problem changed, however,

with the development of oenology and the creation of the first cooperative wineries in 1929–30. Today there are eighteen cooperatives in the region, which handle the vinification of one-third of the total production of the Beaujolais. Their equipment, rudimentary at first, is now thoroughly modern: stainless-steel vats have supplanted concrete ones, allowing the winemakers to achieve complete mastery of temperatures by the manipulation of thermo-regulated systems. The filling and emptying of vats, the transportation of the harvest and the pressing of the grapes is mechanized to the ultimate degree commensurate with a proper respect for the standards imposed by the production of vintage wines.

Today, the wine-grower of the Bas Beaujolais is exclusively a wine-grower. He uses sound vinification methods and produces firmer, slower-developing wines than those of the granitic soils, which acquire all their graces by Easter after the cold winter weather. Once they have shed their original minerality, they exhale a solid, fresh, sappy aroma and their violet-facetted, ruby colour reflects their geological origins. Each year the Beaujolais *appellation* gains ground on the market for new wines, which was once the preserve of Beaujolais-Villages. Created on April 21, 1950, through an administrative simplification of thirty-nine communes and forty-one belltowers (!), Beaujolais-Villages is annually delivered *en primeur* from the end of November onwards. It is light, mischievous and thoroughly drinkable. It is a kind of bridge between the Beaujolais wines discussed above, and the local and commune *cru appellations*. The commercial success of Beaujolais-Villages has never been in doubt since the moment it was created as an *appellation*. The wine trade can count on annual reserves of 300,000 hectolitres, for a total area of over 6200 hectares. In addition, Beaujolais-Villages is something of a technical success story, since to the fifty per cent of regional harvest which leaves the Beaujolais each year it contributes a large proportion. But

let us now move on to a discussion of the *crus*, which are the area's unquestioned ornament.

BROUILLY AND CÔTE-DE-BROUILLY

Quel est donc ce sommet . . .
le bon vin de Brouilly.

These lines by Emile de Villié introduce us to the twin brothers of the Beaujolais family – Brouilly and Côte-de-Brouilly.

From Brouilly to Saint-Amour stretches a sea of short-pruned Gamay vines, ten thousand plants to the hectare, lavishly cared for all through the year. These gnarled and twisted vine stocks have succeeded in pushing their roots into a rock so hard that it successfully resisted the steel implements of quarrymen sent, not long ago, to open up the side of the hill. Mont Brouilly has resisted – and still resists – the onslaught of the centuries, due to the robust nature of its granite and blue-black shale. Mont Brouilly is 485 metres high and stands in the middle of the vineyards, crowned with a chapel built in 1865 and dedicated to Notre-Dame de Fourvières, said to protect the vines against mildew. From the bedroom window in his fine house at Saint-Julien, Claude Bernard saw this chapel being raised and referred to it in a letter to a friend.

Brouilly's vineyards and wines are frequently mentioned and described by authors of former times. Julien, in his 1816 topography of known vineyards, praised the quality of the wines of Odenas and Saint-Lager. In 1857, M Rendu, Inspector-General of Agriculture, situated the 'genuine' Brouilly on the side of Mont Brouilly and called the wine from the area from beyond 'a bastard Brouilly', *Brouilly bâtard*. Nearer our own time, Léon Foillard shows a tendency to place the Brouilly *cru* within the same boundaries and is confirmed in this by different Beaujolais classifications appearing in 1865, 1874, 1891, 1893 . . .

Nonetheless, today's Brouilly *appellation* extends well beyond the limits designated by ancient usage. Let there be no mistake; we do not wish to reignite the quarrel of forty

years ago, which opposed supporters of a purist delineation for the *appellation*, and those – visionaries and opportunists – who preached the extension of Brouilly to include the alluvial soils of its eastern boundary.

Maps dating back to before the tenth century show that place-names ending in *-iacum* were later changed by French into *ié* endings. Thus

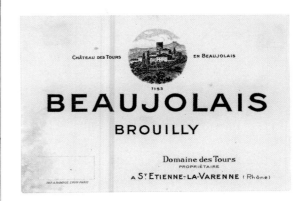

Brulliacum must have become 'Brouillé', not 'Brouilly'. From *brouillé* to *brouille* (quarrel) is only a short step . . .

So we shall confine ourselves to explaining how it is that two *appellations* coexist around Mont Brouilly, without being confused. Both were defined by a decree of October 19, 1938, given their own status, and provided with similar conditions of production. The only difference lies in their geographic location, which for Côtes-de-Brouilly is limited to the slopes of Mont Brouilly and the four communes of Odenas, Saint-Lager, Cercié and Quincié – a total of slightly more than 300 hectares. The present delineation represents the old guard's ideal of a 'Brouilly' appellation. As to straight Brouilly, its preserve covers some of the communes of Mont Brouilly, plus those of Charentay and Saint-Etienne-La-Varenne. Its annual production exceeds 40,000 hectolitres as against 8000 for the Côte. According to a report for the years 1926–34, the total quantity of wine made on Mont Brouilly remained fairly constant, varying between 8000 and 9000 hectolitres. This represents the volume declared at present for the AOC Côte-de-Brouilly. Hence, the extension of 'real' Brouilly required the integration of very diverse soils, ranging from dry granitic to heavy alluvial earth adjoining the plain of the Saône. One readily understands the regrets of those who defended the Côte, like Claude Geoffray – another type of Robespierre likewise defeated by La Plaine.*

At the very heart of the *appellation*, the wines of Côte-de-Brouilly are highly coloured, vigorous, full bodied, and firm. The schistic clay soil bequeaths them their ability (rare in the Beaujolais) to improve with age. The granitic sectors take precedence, producing an increasingly popular table wine. On the edges of the *appellation*, the choices are harder; but both professionals and amateurs will prefer to make their own discoveries and draw their own conclusions . . .

The abundance of *Brouilly* wines ensures them the favour of the wine market, despite their diversity. The

The Madonna of Fleurie. (Painting by G. Cabannes, private collection)

Côte wines, whose characteristics have remained more pronounced and consistent over the years, are less attractive to the industry and often end their careers under their fallback *appellation* of 'Bourgogne'. This is a shame, since they have qualities which should interest a market that is always looking for reliable wine, good for drinking young, but also for keeping. Nonetheless, the Brouilly region preserves a unity which is symbolized by a tasting-cellar at Saint-Lager which is called Cuvage de Brouilly, and much frequented by those lovers of wine and nature who visit the region each year. From the plain to the top of Mont Brouilly, the landscape is studded with beauty spots, *châteaux*, and cool, deep cellars – with names like La Chize, Les Tours, Château-Thivin, Pierreux . . . and during the grape harvest, the hill resembles one great vat, fragrant with the scent of grapes.

*During the French Revolution, La Plaine was a term used to define the moderates in the National Convention who brought down Robespierre.

CHIROUBLES

When the appearance of the dreaded greenfly, *puceron*, was reported for the first time in 1865 at Roquemaure, in the Gard, Victor Pulliat had already been living thirty-eight years at Chiroubles, in the heart of the Beaujolais.

The name of Victor Pulliat features with those of Millardet, Foex, Viala, Ravaz and Planchon as one of those

scientists who saved the vineyards of France from total destruction by phylloxera. Pulliat played his part first on a local, then a worldwide stage. At his domaine of Temperé, he assembled a collection of over two thousand vine varieties, from the study of which he established a scale of precocity which is still a basic reference for all ampelographers. On his death in 1896, he was probably unaware that the village of his birth would one day carry the reputation of its wine far beyond the borders of the Beaujolais.

Chiroubles, nestling in its granite amphitheatre, at 400 metres altitude, is the first communal entity we encounter in our review of the Beaujolais. The village is built closely around a twelfth-century church, as if to leave as much room as possible for the vineyards which crowd in on it from every quarter. It marks the centre of an area that climbs westward to the slopes of Mont Avenas (700 metres).

Just as the vines of Chiroubles belong to a single variety, so the soil of the commune is of a single type: the coarse granite of the Massif de Fleurie, with occasional patches of granulite earth. The rock, under the combined assault of man and weather, has been gradually worn away, leaving a meagre sandy topsoil which is only good for vines.

The geometrical parcels of land here are separated by ancient walls, built of stones prised out of the ground with iron bars by generations of men.

Along these steep slopes punctuated by sheer drops, the motorized winch is the ideal implement for bringing up both trenching ploughs and the soil, which is often washed off the bare rock by storms.

Light, thin, acid and porous, the soil of the Chiroubles vineyards fulfils all the conditions required to produce quality wines within the territorial limits fixed by the decree of September 11, 1936, which defines the *appellation contrôlée* Chiroubles.

While official recognition did not immediately lead to popular consecration, the merits of the commune's wines were far from unknown to local dealers. We possess a list of tariffs dated December 30, 1879, on which the wines of Chiroubles are priced according to their vintage:

	1874	1876	1877	1878
	(Francs)			
First choice	300	185	135	140
Second choice	280	160	125	120–135

These are prices for two hundred and fifteen-litre casks. By way of comparison, the same vintages from Moulin-à-Vent were sold at 360, 230, 160, 180 francs. Thus Chiroubles was already competing favourably with the *cru* which is generally considered to be the best in the Beaujolais. Certain authors have seen in Chiroubles the intermediate wine – or link – between Fleurie and Morgon. Chiroubles, it is said, has Fleurie's charm and Morgon's solidity. In fact, the qualities of Chiroubles are uniquely its own, even though on the edges of the commune bordering Fleurie, or other *appellations*, these qualities can be confused. At its heart, it is completely distinctive.

The first visitors to the Maison des Beaujolais were immediately impressed with Chiroubles and from the very beginning it ranked first in the approval ratings of all the *appellations* offered for tasting. We do not know if this is still the case, but at all events, its early success has contributed to the *appellation*'s subsequent vigour.

On July 14, 1953, the Terrasse des Chiroubles was inaugurated on the Fût d'Avenas, complete with an orientation table and the blessing of local officials. The craze for publicity had begun to affect the vineyards and Chiroubles followed Villié Morgon as a pioneer in the field, showing how goodwill could triumph against all obstacles (including lack of money).

Since then, Chiroubles has come a long way. From the communal chalet built in 1958, the visitor can view practically all the 345 hectares of the *appellation*, which produce an average of 13,000 hectolitres of wine each year. The cooperative winery also possesses its own tasting-cellar, so all in all, the *cru* has a particularly strong marketing infrastructure.

It is a fact that Chiroubles, with its elegance, finesse, and scent of violets, is best drunk young – despite declarations to the contrary by oenologists. The very nature of the soil lends itself to the creation of wines with a rich, flowery aroma, short on tannin and colour and drinkable soon after the harvest. There are some *cuvées* which may be kept longer; these are either left to ferment longer in the vat or come from the higher vineyards. Served cool, Chiroubles can be served from the beginning to the end of a meal; as they say, it 'slips down the throat like Jesus in velvet trousers'.

FLEURIE

In 1722, a deputy from the Mâconnais to the States-General of Burgundy declared that the share of the Beaujolais wine production sent up to Paris should be limited to two or three superior *crus*: those of Chénas, Fleurie and Saint-Lager. Thus Fleurie's viticultural antecedents are old indeed.

Chiroubles

APPELLATION CONTROLÉE

J. LABROSSE-LORIN
VINS FINS, BELLEVILLE-s/-SAÔNE (RHÔNE)

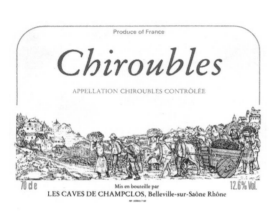

Produce of France

Chiroubles

APPELLATION CHIROUBLES CONTRÔLÉE

70 cle   Mis en bouteille par   12.6% Vol.
LES CAVES DE CHAMPCLOS, Belleville-sur-Saône Rhône

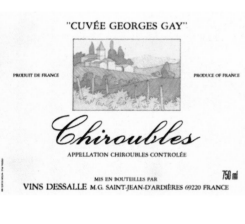

"CUVÉE GEORGES GAY"

PRODUIT DE FRANCE   PRODUCE OF FRANCE

Chiroubles

APPELLATION CHIROUBLES CONTRÔLÉE

MIS EN BOUTEILLES PAR   750 ml
VINS DESSALLE M.G. SAINT-JEAN-D'ARDIÈRES 69220 FRANCE

SAINT-AMOUR
APPELLATION SAINT-AMOUR CONTRÔLÉE

MIS EN BOUTEILLES PAR LES PRODUCTEURS RÉUNIS

MAISON DU VIGNERON
QUINCIÉ (RHONE) FRANCE   e 750 ml
PRODUIT DE FRANCE

Fleurie, au nom joli comme un printemps nouveau, says the poet. In the range of Beaujolais wines, this *cru* has a very special place of its own; even though its *appellation*, which dates from September 11, 1936 does not distinguish it from the others.

The Massif de Fleurie is geologically composed of granite containing large crystal formations. In its higher, steeper areas, at the foot of the Vierge Noire, the weathered rock harbours a thin layer of sandy soil to which the vines cling. Their roots penetrate the slightest cracks in the stone, from which they draw the elements that characterize the wines of Fleurie.

The poor, sandy soil offers an excellent situation for vines and produces wine of great quality. In their classification table for the *crus* of the Beaujolais, David and Foillard define Fleurie wines as very pleasing, agreeably constructed and with much strength and flavour despite their apparent lightness.

This general verdict does not fully satisfy the oenologists. In the eastern part of the commune, well above the village, the soil is enriched by rain-borne alluvial deposits from the hill-top; the depth of the earth increases along with the rising proportions of clay. The slope is disappearing, cultivation is growing easier and productivity is increasing. The wines of this zone are highly coloured and well structured, gaining in body and longevity what they lost initially in finesse.

Thus the 780 hectares of Fleurie produce a range of different wines, some to be drunk young, others capable of ageing several years in a cellar. Whether it is drunk soon or late, this *cru* owes its fame to its consistent quality and its confirmed bouquet of iris, amber and violets. Elegant and restrained, a blend of grace and harmony, Fleurie is always out of the ordinary. With a yearly production that hovers between 42,000 and 45,000 hectolitres, it is the region's third largest communal producer, after Brouilly and Morgon. Part of the harvest is made into wine by the cooperative, which stands at the centre of the village and attracts many Sunday visitors.

Like the other cooperatives, the Cave des Grands Vins de Fleurie has always stressed quality, achieved by careful selection of grapes, strict control over the ripening fruit and modernization of vinification equipment. This has entailed considerable investments. The president, Mlle Chabert – 'Marguerite' to her friends – continues the work of her father, a pork butcher by trade, who started the cooperative. She likes to say that her nephew, also a pork butcher, *fait l'andouille*, to remind everyone that her father invented an andouillette sausage which has become almost as famous as the local wine.

Fleurie has many fine houses and *châteaux*, but no one very famous or glorious seems to have lived here at any time. The Fleuriatons are perhaps mindful of this shortage of distinguished ancestors and it spurs them to special efforts. Anything could happen today at Fleurie-la-Belle . . . in fact, one of the songs in Marguerite Chabert's repertoire prophesies that Fleurie will one day be the county town of the district – even the regional sub-prefecture – maybe even the capital of France. The Elysée Palace at Fleurie? Well, in the meantime, we can wager that Fleurie will continue to feature strongly – in the cellars of the President of the Republic.

MORGON

Villié-Morgon has always been an attractive, and active, centre. During the French Revolution, it was even a county town of the district, but without Morgon. By an act (No 999) registered on April 25, 1867 at the Prefecture of the Rhône, Napoleon

The village of Chénas

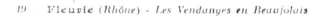

MORGON

APPELLATION CONTROLÉE

CHOISI POUR VOUS PAR PAUL BLANC
AU CHAPON FIN A THOISSEY, AIN

'by the grace of God and by the will of the people, Emperor of the French' decreed the union which attached the administrative centre of Villié (formerly spelt Villiers) to the well-known patronym of Morgon.

Without reawakening the quarrel over which is the oldest vineyard in the Beaujolais, we may note that Morgon, like Juliénas and Brouilly, is mentioned as a vineyard area as early as the tenth century. An act dated 956, whereby the Sire de Beaujeu sold a vineyard to one of his vassals, supports this thesis. The vines of Morgon, which covered 723 hectares in 1892, now extend over 1000 hectares.

The heart of the *cru* draws its organoleptic originality and its special suitability for ageing from the *morgons*, crumbling rocks produced by the breakdown (under the effects of weather and cultivation implements) of pyritic shale. The latter is made up of ancient deposits impregnated with iron oxides, which colour the earth ochre and the wine a garnet-red. The essence of this ground is to be found at the Py de Morgon, a gently sloping breast-shaped hill from which there flows *un lait incomparable et pur*, as Emile de Villié has written.

The wines of Morgon have always held a special place in the classifications, because of their richness of dry extract and their generous colour, which make them better for ageing than most of the other regional *crus*. Certain authors do not hesitate to state that Morgons can be kept for a decade or longer. This would, of course, be taking the exception for the rule; in fact, a good vintage lasted four or five years, keeping its original characteristics and its commercial value. I say 'lasted', because today, in many cases, this is no longer true. The marketing of younger and younger wines has made traditional vinification a rarity. It took elaborate processes to produce that raspberry-flavoured Morgon with the aroma of kirsch; that robust, powerful and general wine which was reproached by some for being '. . . too Burgundy, and not Beaujolais enough!'

Wine derives a characteristic tang from its soil, and short fermentation prevents the nature of the soil from affecting the wine.

The true vocation of Morgon is not the production of young wine, but of quality wine that can be kept a while and drunk to accompany red meat and cheese. The wine-growers are just as convinced of this as we are, and they are already quietly correcting their course. To define their wines, they prefer a single image to a crowd of superlatives, and have invented the all-purpose verb *morgonner* to describe what they do. '*Morgonner*' is a sovereign cure for the grumps and the dumps, and the Villiatons had plenty of those during the Revolution, when the sire Mignot de Bussy led a plot to save Louis XVI from the clutches of the *Révolutionnaires*. Louis Capet lost his head, but Bussy saved his, emigrated to Austria, and was even compensated after the Restoration. But his *château* and his vines (which extended from Lacenas to Juliénas) were sold off as the property of the nation. The vineyard was broken up and the Château de Fontcrenne was bought by one M Gaudet. In 1921, M Joubert, the mayor of Villié-Morgon, bought the park and buildings for the municipality.

Ever since 1953, the cellars of the *château* have been used for the Caveau de Morgon, the first of a line of tasting-cellars which have greatly contributed toward making the Beaujolais better known to tourists.

As for the vines, they still adorn the slopes with their seasonal colours, yielding each autumn the same good wine which transcends ideas to remain the true symbol of joy and truth.

MOULIN-À-VENT

At Romanèche-Thorins, known to the Romans as Matronis Romaniscis, a venerable windmill overlooks the vines; it has been abandoned by the miller, but it remains a beacon for the lost traveller in the realm of Bacchus. Moulin-à-Vent is the noblest *cru* of the Beaujolais, comparable to the great wines of Burgundy. Here we cross the administrative boundary into the region of the Rhône, a boundary straddled by the *appellation*; for the grapes of Moulin-à-Vent are

also harvested at Chénas, without, for all that, causing any dissension, since it was the wine-growers of Moulin-à-Vent who first preached the unity which is the great strength of the Beaujolais region today. At the turn of the century, Chénas wine-growers were already selling their wine under the *appellation* Thorins, the name of the place where the famous windmill stands, and which was merged with Romanèche in 1860 at the latter's request.

By 1921, the wine-growers of Chénas and Romanèche were engaged in frontal warfare, instigated by M Méziat, the mayor of Chénas.

After a series of court cases, a judgement handed down at Mâcon on April 17, 1924, finally fixed the limits of Moulin-à-Vent, which thereby became the oldest *cru* in the Beaujolais. The decrees of 1936 defining the AOC wines confirmed this first decision.

The vineyards grow on a shallow terrain of friable, disintegrated, salmon-pink granite, and the presence of manganese in this soil adds class to the bouquet of these pedigree wines. Moulin-à-Vent is also credited with longevity; indeed, it is often classed with Burgundies on restaurant wine lists. In the old days,

Burgundian wine-growers used to come to make the Moulin-à-Vent wines themselves, producing a solid, well-structured product which could not be drunk before it was three years old. What was it like? Around the time of the phylloxera in 1880, an old wine-grower described what he remembered:

'To make the Moulin-à-Vent of my ancestors, you needed velvet, miles of velvet, and piles of rubies, and scented flowers and delicious fruits. To make the Moulin-à-Vent of my ancestors, you needed the rays of the sun, the soft flicker of a wood fire, and fine music. You needed the bodies of beautiful women . . . and you needed all these things at the same time. Only our old gamay vines could perform such a miracle!'

The clear-juiced black Gamay, grafted, pruned and cherished, yields the same velvety wine each year. In accordance with the taste of the day, it is drunk relatively young, thanks to shorter, more flexible vinification techniques. But this does not keep Moulin-à-Vent from being a wine that improves with age. Whether it is drunk young, adolescent or old, it remains the undisputed seigneur of the Beaujolais.

CHÉNAS

The legend of Chénas somewhat resembles one of Perrault's fairytales:

'The mediaeval forest stretched all over the slopes of Chénas. A band of woodcutters lived and worked in the surrounding hills. One of these woodcutters, noticing that the granite soil was suitable for growing vines, called on the nobles of the place to

The famous moulin *overlooking the vines*

BENOÎT RACLET, SAVIOUR OF THE VINES

For many years, the vines of the Beaujolais were devastated by pyralis. Léon Foillard, in his excellent book, describes the full extent of the disaster:

'The area affected covered some 4500 hectares; 2000 in the Saône-et-Loire, and 2500 in the Rhône. Then the plague spread throughout the Beaujolais and the Mâconnais and into other wine regions, always seeming to prefer red grapes to white. Perpetual winter gripped the districts of Romanèche, Saint-Amour, La Chapelle and Chénas. . . .'

The wine-growers talked of burning the vines which had been overwhelmed by the 'rascal worm'. They no longer believed in anything. A pilgrimage had been organized to 'Notre-Dame-du-Ver', the old Chapelle des Minimes at Montmerle; but when they were caught unawares by a violent thunderstorm while crossing the Saône in boats, the pilgrims had lost all hope. The Madonna was installed at Avenas, whence she disappeared soon after . . . for ever.

Benoît Raclet, the son of a Roanne attorney, nineteenth in a family of twenty-seven children and living at Romanèche-Thorins since his marriage, happened to notice that the vine beside his house on which the hot dishwater was emptied every day, remained in excellent health. He concluded that the surest and simplest way of destroying pyralis must consist in pouring boiling water, échaudage, over the vines during the winter.

For more than ten years, Raclet experimented on his vineyard at Breneys, applying rigorous scientific methods. Not only was he not taken seriously, but the innovator was accused of wishing to kill the vines with his cauldrons of water. The 'cauldron carriers', échaudeurs, were obliged to take ferocious dogs with them when they worked at night. Mortified and discouraged, Benoît

Raclet abandoned his experiments, then resumed them and finally triumphed over the sceptics.

Pyralis was defeated, but Benoît Raclet, ruined and semi-paralysed, retired to the Charolais, where he died on March 31, 1844. His invention had brought him the Legion of Honour, but alas, the cross could only be placed on his coffin.

For a century, the method of échaudage protected the vines of France, and whilst it was still being used in the years 1939–40, it disappeared completely around 1945 with the arrival of new insecticides.

'The inventor is a long-range benefactor', said Lamartine. Public recognition perhaps takes a long time to manifest itself, but at least it is perpetuated from generation to generation. A monument to Benoît Raclet was erected at Romanèche in 1864, and every year since then, on the last Sunday of October, the wine-growers compare their Beaujolais Nouveaux at a great exhibition which is simply known as the 'Fête Raclet'. During this fête, schoolchildren solemnly sing a cantata composed by the poet Grégoire Dessaigne and dedicated to the saviour of the vines:

« Que tous les ans pour la vendange
la foule vienne chaque soir
de Raclet chanter la louange
aux accords bruyants du pressoir,
et qu'en rond, sur toute la ligne,
ce même chant soit répété :
Si bon Noé planta la vigne,
Lui, sauva l'arbre de Noé. »

tear up the oaks that made up the great forest.

'A royal ordinance, dated 1321 and remitted by the lord of that province, gave the right to uproot the oaks and set vines in their stead. When the trees had gone, the woodcutter gave the name of Chénas to the place where his first vines were planted, in memory of the oaks which were there before; and he gave the vines the name of Gamay, in memory of the first tune they prompted him to sing.'

Charming, but not necessarily true. While most writers agree that the name of Chénas designated a place planted with oak trees, and that the countryside was once covered with forest, the seventeenth-century historian Baluze records that a capitulary of Charlemagne ordered the land to be cleared. So who was it who gave permission for vines to be grown? Was it the emperor, or Philip the Tall, the 'accursed king'?

Let us leave the historians to dispute this and move on to Chénas itself, the smallest *cru* in the Beaujolais.

The old village stands with its back to the Pic Raymond, built, according to legend, by Gargantua when he

The vineyard at the old Domaine de Chénas. (Anon, private collection)

116

PALAIS DU COMMERCE

MAISON HENRI IV

BANQUET DU 11 JUIN 1911

CAILLES LUCULLUS
SAUMON BRAISÉ Sce NANTUA
SELLE DE PRÉ SALÉ PARISIENNE
CÈPES BORDELAISE
PINTADONS TRUFFÉS
PATÉ DE STRASBOURG
ASPERGES EN BRANCHES

✠ ✠ ✠

GLACE PLOMBIÈRES   VINS
DESSERT

⚜ ⚜   CHÉNAS EN CARAFES
                      CHATEAU LA TOUR BLANCHE
                      CHATEAU CITRAN
                      POMMARD
                      WHITE-STAR
                      ⚜

Servi par
WATTEBLED & Cie

FONTAINE BARTHOLDI

Imp B ARNAUD LYON PARIS

emptied his pannier of grapes. The commune is made up of several small hamlets, each with different soils, though all are more or less granitic.

As we have seen, the wine-growers of Chénas were at the origin of Moulin-à-Vent. Thus Chénas has the distinction of possessing two *crus* on its territory, its own, and that of Moulin-à-Vent. Though not related, the two *crus* remain allies, the more so since Chénas flirts with the Saône-et-Loire by extending its *appellation* area across the best slopes of La Chapelle-de-Guinchay. It is said of Chénas that it is 'a bunch of flowers in a velvet basket'. Real lovers of distinctive Beaujolais revere this celebratory wine, which has many points of similarity with Burgundy and was said to have honoured the table of Louis XIII. Because of its modesty and discretion, Chénas probably does not occupy its rightful place in the hierarchy of Beaujolais *appellations*. Perhaps this is because its production area is so limited.

The Chénas tasting-cellar, which stands beside the Route du Beaujolais, possesses a number of historic treasures. It has the intimate atmosphere of a typical local village; and it was once administrated by M Le Haute (former chief tax official of the Beaujolais) who bequeathed to the cooperative of Chénas the finest vaulted cellars in the region.

JULIÉNAS

Juliénas, at the northernmost point of the Beaujolais, stands astride the

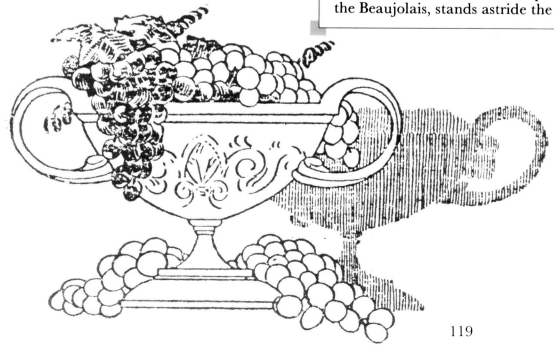

place where Gamay vines end and Chardonnays begin. This choice – and adaptation – of varieties which differ both in colour and disposition, may be explained by the prevalent geological formations and the nature of the resultant soils.

At Juliénas, granite makes way for second-era formations; ancient alluvial deposits, hence deeper, richer soils. Of course, the change is not an abrupt one, since soil layers do not split like schistic slate. Cultivation and erosion have created a smooth blend of earth which is particularly suitable for vines. The fame of Juliénas, outside its connections with the newspaper world, may rest on the fact that grapes were growing here when the rest of the Beaujolais was still a forest – a fact attested by many reliable documents. How did vines come to Juliénas before they reached the easternmost slopes of the region? This remains a mystery.

The commune of Juliénas, spelt 'Julliénas' until the end of the nineteenth century, lies within the district of Beaujeu. It became an *appellation controlée* by a decree of March 11, 1938. The area delimited covers four communes, with an incursion into the Saône-et-Loire. At first, the total AOC area covered 530 hectares 96 ares 99 centiares (note the precision), with 436 h 05 a 38 ca at Juliénas; 2 h 18 a 05 ca at Emeringues; 67 h 84 a 96 ca at Jullié; and 24 h 88a 60 ca at Pruzilly. Since then, certain complementary surveys have increased this area to a little

over 560 hectares. Because they are so close to the clay soils of the Mâconnais, the vineyards of Juliénas give to their wines a deep, intense, ruby colour and plenty of dry matter. This allows them to age very well in certain vintages.

Wines from Jullié and Emeringues are probably less suitable for ageing. We say 'probably', because here, as everywhere else in the Beaujolais, the diversity of soils, expositions, altitude and people lead to wide contrasts.

The wine-growers of Juliénas well know how to take advantage of modern oenological methods, whether they make their own wine from their own harvest, or whether they rely on the cooperative cellars (built in 1960).

In 1660, at Bois de la Salle, Mathieu Gayot, Treasurer of France, built a priory which later became the property of the Sieur Charrier, who in turn built the *château* which today contains the cellars of the *grands vins de* Juliénas. We note in passing that at one time Juliénas was dependent on the chapter of Saint-Vincent-lès-Mâcon, which levied the ecclesiastical tithe on the commune: that is, a tenth part of the land tax imposed. The Revolution abolished this tax, and all that remains of it now is a five-galleried house known as Maison de la Dîme, or des Dîmes, containing the strongroom used by the collectors for storing the tax money. As a former fief of the lords of Beaujeu, Juliénas had many chapels and *châteaux*. Among these was the Château de

Juliénas, which has some of the finest old cellars in the Beaujolais. Its present owner, while he is not the seigneur of the Beaujolais, nonetheless presides over the Cellier de la Vielle Eglise, a tasting-cellar set up in 1955 in an unused chapel. The building has been redecorated by a Paris painter, in a style inspired by the surrounding area; thus the chancel is packed with leaping fawns, impassioned nymphs, rubicund Bacchuses and facetious cherubs. These delightful figures are as charming as the wine of Juliénas, and only an idiot or a teetotaller could be shocked by them.

The Cellier was originally founded by Victor Peyret, who died all too young. His memory is preserved by his friends and successors in the form of a prize, given annually to an artist, painter, journalist, writer or designer who has served the cause of Juliénas. The fortunate winner of this prize is presented with one hundred and four bottles of the best *cru*, amid scenes of much gaiety and festivity.

SAINT-AMOUR

At the extreme northern limit of the region lies Saint-Amour, last of the Beaujolais *crus*. The name Saint-Amour is derived from Saint Amateur, a Roman soldier who was converted to Christianity and founded a monastery on a mountain peak overlooking the river Saône. The story of Saint-Amour is similar to those of many other Beaujolais

Domaine de la Maison de la Dime. (G. Cabannes, private collection)

A 'VIN NOUVEAU' CURE AT JULIÉNAS

An historic day . . .

On September 29, Le Canard Enchaîné is received by its friends and loyal readers, the wine-growers of Juliénas. Juliénas! A name to be remembered and put in bottles. As to the wine-growers, they wear their hearts on their sleeves.

Ten o'clock.

Hillsides; warm, welcoming houses; surrounding vines with foliage turning red in the autumn sunshine; and good friends to greet us.

The time spent on formalities is kept to a minimum.

Straight away, we get down to essentials.

'Mind the steps!'

We're in a cellar. Two cellars. Lots of cellars.

'You're at Juliénas!'

Juliénas starts with everything I mentioned above – hillsides welcoming homes, vineleaves turning red; but it ends with a cellar.

The rest is only secondary.

The tour of the cellars follows a careful ritual. First you are shown the lines of casks; then a small recipient is put into your hands.

'There's your tasse!'

This is for tasting the wine.

When we have tasted this year's wine, we have to taste last year's, then the year's before, and so on; then a wine which has a particular type of fruitiness, then another which, though it is less fruity than the most fruity, is nonetheless fruitier than the least fruity, then . . .

It's when you come out of the cellar that the warning should be heeded.

'Mind the steps!'

Strange, there seem to be more than before!

From an article by Jules Rivet, *Canard Enchaîné*, Autumn 1934

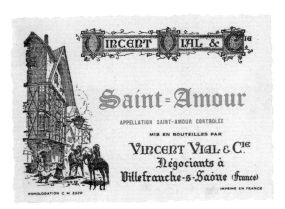

commenced. An early prosperity, cut short by the appearance of phylloxera; then wrecked in the years after 1914–18, while the landscape burgeoned with monuments to those killed in the war. The slump in wines in the first years of the century also accelerated a population exodus: a cask cost twenty-five francs at the cooper's, and its contents were worth only twelve francs! Strong arms to wield the mattock or carry the can of sulphate were hard to come by. During the Gallo-Roman era, the people of Saint-Amour numbered around 2000; at the armistice, in 1918, this total had fallen to less than 450.

Today, the population is again on the increase and the status of *appellation contrôlée* has had a lot to do with this phenomenon.

The *Saint-Amour appellation* is the youngest of the nine *crus* of the Beaujolais. It was born in 1946, two years after the others, and it owes everything to the faith and passion of one of its children – Louis Dailly.

The commune lies at the juncture of the granitic zone (with its vocation for fine red wines), and the limestone favoured by the Chardonnay grape. Chardonnay is used to make quality whites such as Mâcon and Saint-Véran. From 275 hectares planted with vines inside the designated area, the average annual wine yield is between 8500 and 9000 hectolitres – all of which goes to satisfy the ever-growing demand for Saint-Amour in France and abroad. The decalcified 'Beaujolais' sector of the *appellation* is made up of clay-silica soils, with clay elements surrounding rocky or pebbly particles which have separated from the granitic bedrock and arkose

(Triassic sandstone). These soils produce highly coloured, solid, substantial wines, which are rich in tannin and may be kept as long as Morgons and Juliénas.

For commercial reasons, and in order to ensure a rapid turnover, some growers here apply *vin nouveau* technology and produce lighter-coloured wines to be drunk young. We believe that they are mistaken and that Saint-Amour, like the other *crus* (with the possible exception of Chiroubles) should confine itself to producing wines for bottling and for the restaurant market.

When properly made and bottled at the right time, Saint-Amours offer all the fruitiness of the Gamay grape, and lose nothing of their distinctiveness. They can always be relied upon as a fit accompaniment to roasts, game and the cheeses of the Beaujolais hills. If anyone needs convincing of the real quality of Saint-Amour, he need only come to taste the selection offered by the Caveau des Saint-Amour, which has operated since 1965 in a converted garage. This building has been completely altered, adapted to tasting needs and decorated by the Lyon-based painter Nicolas Janin with frescoes and scenes of the grape harvest. So nothing has been lost . . . and Saint-Amour hopes soon to expand its *appellation* by a few dozen hectares, the better to satisfy its loyal customers.

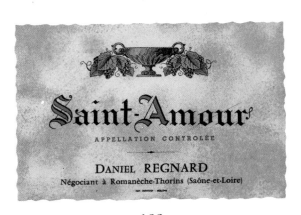

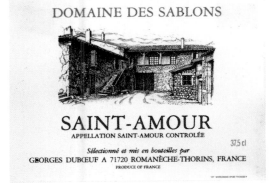

The village of Saint-Amour-Bellevue

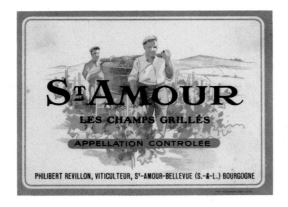

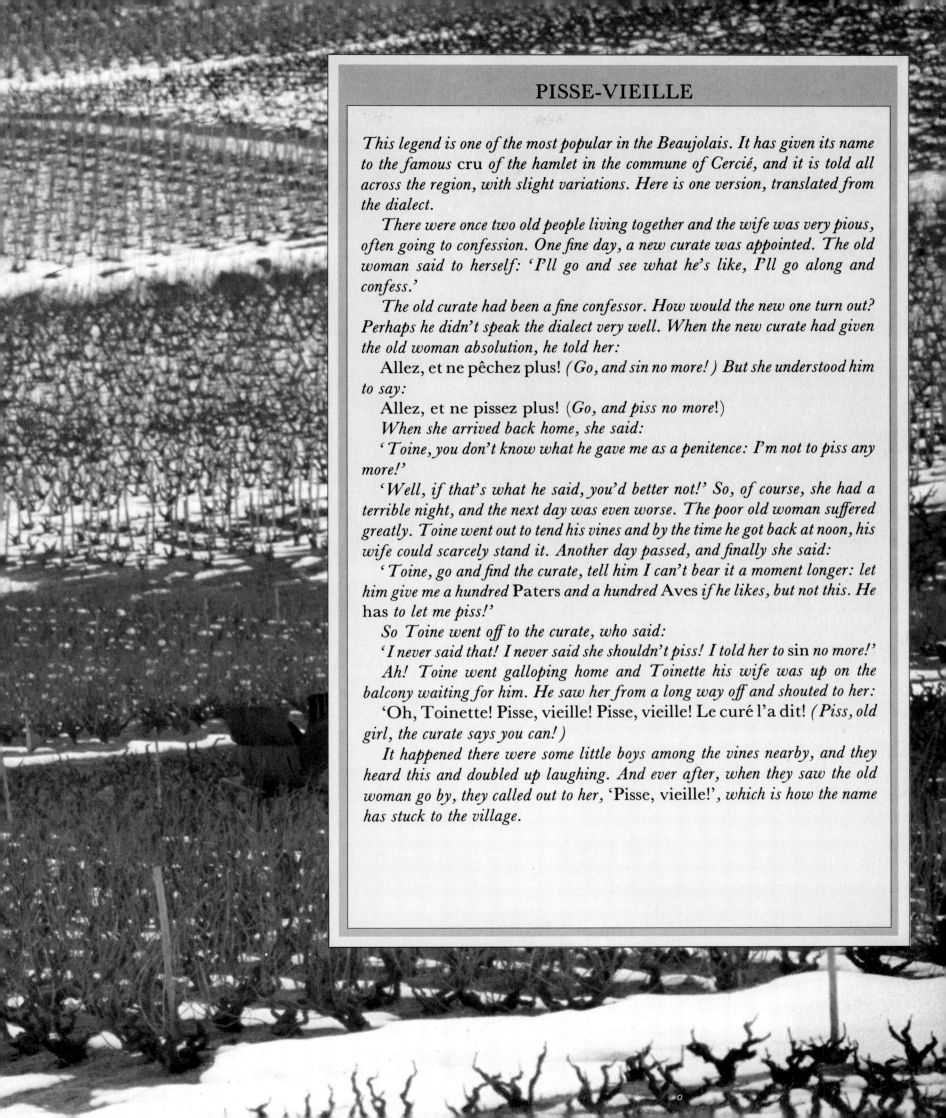

PISSE-VIEILLE

This legend is one of the most popular in the Beaujolais. It has given its name to the famous cru *of the hamlet in the commune of Cercié, and it is told all across the region, with slight variations. Here is one version, translated from the dialect.*

There were once two old people living together and the wife was very pious, often going to confession. One fine day, a new curate was appointed. The old woman said to herself: 'I'll go and see what he's like, I'll go along and confess.'

The old curate had been a fine confessor. How would the new one turn out? Perhaps he didn't speak the dialect very well. When the new curate had given the old woman absolution, he told her:

Allez, et ne pêchez plus! *(Go, and sin no more!)* But she understood him to say:

Allez, et ne pissez plus! *(Go, and piss no more!)*

When she arrived back home, she said:

'Toine, you don't know what he gave me as a penitence: I'm not to piss any more!'

'Well, if that's what he said, you'd better not!' So, of course, she had a terrible night, and the next day was even worse. The poor old woman suffered greatly. Toine went out to tend his vines and by the time he got back at noon, his wife could scarcely stand it. Another day passed, and finally she said:

'Toine, go and find the curate, tell him I can't bear it a moment longer: let him give me a hundred Paters and a hundred Aves if he likes, but not this. He has to let me piss!'

So Toine went off to the curate, who said:

'I never said that! I never said she shouldn't piss! I told her to sin no more!'

Ah! Toine went galloping home and Toinette his wife was up on the balcony waiting for him. He saw her from a long way off and shouted to her:

'Oh, Toinette! Pisse, vieille! Pisse, vieille! Le curé l'a dit! *(Piss, old girl, the curate says you can!)*

It happened there were some little boys among the vines nearby, and they heard this and doubled up laughing. And ever after, when they saw the old woman go by, they called out to her, 'Pisse, vieille!', which is how the name has stuck to the village.

Vintages

Gaston CHARLE

Nature, who is kind and cruel by turns, and man, who tries to correct her caprices, each year combine their forces to create original wines. From one harvest to the next, wine changes its fundamental characteristics, modifying its evolution, and varying its expectation of life. As evidence of this perpetual diversity, here is a breakdown of Beaujolais vintages over the last twenty-six years.

1960: Despite unfavourable weather, this vintage produced a few good growths; fruity, well coloured, but to be drunk early.

1961: Very good quality. Fine colour, good balance between body and alcoholic content, and fruity flavour – these were the distinctive characteristics of this vintage, which was an immediate commercial success. In the *crus*, as in the south of the Beaujolais, the wines were full, firm and suitable for ageing.

1962: This vintage was generally satisfactory. The *primeurs* were successful in their allotted areas: on granitic soils. Wines from the clay-limestone districts were aggressive for a certain length of time. The '62s were wines of character.

1963: The harvest this year was late, only beginning on October 5. '63s proved to be *primeurs* rather than *vins de garde* (for keeping); they reminded some (nostalgic) people of the wines

of yesteryear, *les petits beaujolais des bistrots lyonnais*.

1964: By contrast with the preceding year, 1964 was exceedingly dry. All the skill of the wine-grower was necessary to obtain a successful result, which came in the form of wines conforming to type in the *crus*. '64s will keep well.

1965: To use a local expression, this was an *année pourrie* (a rotten year), which resulted in carafe-type wines, light and for rapid consumption.

1966: Thanks to a warm autumn which greatly assisted the ripening of the grapes, this year's wines proved to be healthy and drinkable.

1967: This vintage was an all-round year, both for carafe wines, produced in the granitic areas, and for characteristic *crus*. In general, the wines produced were well balanced, supple and full bodied. Their colour was not particularly strong, but the tone of it was a fine cherry-red.

1968: The vintage was much affected by heavy rain. Only the *primeur* wines were constant in quality in this difficult year.

1969: A year that began with a number of problems (few grapes, washing away of pollen by spring rains, hailstorms), 1969 ended by producing quality wines by virtue of a fine autumn. The wines proved well constructed and full bodied. Their colour was brilliant, a gleaming red, and the *crus* were able to make wines for laying down such as had not been seen since 1961.

1970: The 1970 production exceeded one million hectolitres. A healthy harvest, well ripened from the end of September onward, gave very agreeable, well constituted, and well balanced wines. This impression was confirmed by a very active demand for *primeurs*, which for the first time exceeded 100,000 hectolitres.

Tricentenary bottle:
Château de la Chaize

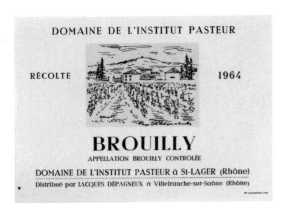

DOMAINE DE L'INSTITUT PASTEUR

RÉCOLTE 1964

BROUILLY

APPELLATION BROUILLY CONTRÔLÉE

DOMAINE DE L'INSTITUT PASTEUR à St-LAGER (Rhône)

Distribué par JACQUES DÉPAGNEUX à Villefranche-sur-Saône (Rhône)

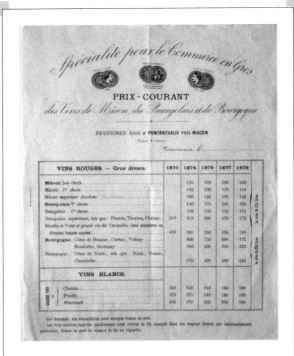

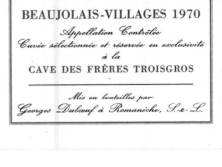

BEAUJOLAIS-VILLAGES 1970

Appellation Contrôlée

Cuvée sélectionnée et réservée en exclusivité
à la

CAVE DES FRÈRES TROISGROS

Mis en bouteilles par

Georges Dubœuf à Romanèche, S.-&-L.

1971: The saccharine richness of the first grapes brought in were a surprise to the growers, who were unused to such strong musts, often attaining eleven or twelve degrees. The wines of this vintage were generally well constructed, rich in dry elements and alcoholic – but they lacked colour and fruitiness.

1972: Due to a late (and sometimes difficult) ripening of the grapes, the wines of 1972 were unsuitable for *primeur* treatment. On the other hand, the *crus* improved as the months went by and developed a good lively colour and body; thus they turned out well in the end.

1973: This vintage was remarkable for its superabundant harvest, which set a record for the time. However, some exceptional growths emerged from the pack, as usual. These were from grapes that were harvested late and which had consequently benefited from a fine October.

1974: After a period of drought, the rain which fell on the night of August 30 was very welcome. Sadly, rain continued throughout September, and October was no better. In the end, the wines turned out heavily coloured and agreeable, though without much fruit to them. They finished much better than might have been expected from the quality shown by the *primeurs*.

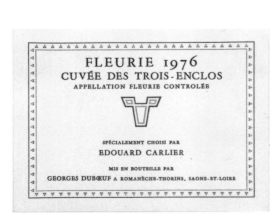

FLEURIE 1976
CUVÉE DES TROIS-ENCLOS
APPELLATION FLEURIE CONTRÔLÉE

SPÉCIALEMENT CHOISI PAR
EDOUARD CARLIER

MIS EN BOUTEILLE PAR
GEORGES DUBŒUF A ROMANÈCHE-THORINS, SAONE-ET-LOIRE

PRODUCE OF FRANCE
HEDIARD
21, Place de la Madeleine, Paris

1979

SAINT AMOUR

Appellation Contrôlée

Mis en bouteille par HEDIARD
à St-Georges-de-Reneins (Rhône) France   750 ml

1947 AND 1949: TWO EXCEPTIONAL VINTAGES

The wine of 1947? Add a little blue to the landscape. And put in some light. During the lifetime of this almanach — first number in 1931, and still going strong, thanks to our Beaujolais-loving editor — the writer of this column has had the pleasure of celebrating many a wine, from many a year. The 'Victory Wine' of 1945 was not the least of them. But 1947 is 'The Glorious'. Thanks be to our Beaujolais vineyards (and our hard-working wine-growers) — we can put out the flags, toss flowers, search the dictionary for the most extravagant compliments in the language. We can go back thirty-five, forty years in the annals of the Beaujolais — maybe even further. There has been nothing like this. Briefly (because we could write whole books describing and ennumerating all the qualities of 1947), let us say that the wine of this year has everything that denotes a very great vintage, along with a few other qualities which we may discover, if we linger. It has been called delicate, even figuratively delicate; but so is any work of art that is brought to absolute perfection.

In 1949, the very fine weather repelled all diseases and malevolent insects from our vineyard slopes. There were a few almost unbearable evenings, when we expected the heavy skies to open. But in the end, there were only a few short hailstorms, which struck in very limited areas and without any catastrophic effect. Above all, the vines stood up famously. The harvest was highly satisfactory; deep soils yielded normal volumes, even in the grands crus; while the lighter, sandy ground, which is always more vulnerable to bad weather, proved generous to its owners.

The wine this year is exceptional. Very fruity, perhaps a little full bodied in some growths, but always worthy of great praise. 1949 will go down in the annals of the Beaujolais as one of the great years, which people will remember and talk about at length, for a long time to come, around tables littered with bottles. According to an old lover of Beaujolais, who is thoroughly knowledgeable on all aspects of the subject, one would have to go back to 1863 to find wines of a quality resembling the nectar which we can savour today.

Extracts from the *Almanach du Beaujolais*, 1948 and 1950

1975: The rot was very prevalent during the season and some wines were attacked by casse. The first to emerge were alcoholic, sometimes a trifle too firm; they were also aggressively acidic and lacked colour. As the year progressed, some good *cuvées* appeared, but in the end the vintage did not fulfil its early promise.

1976: This year, the harvest came very early, beginning in the first days of September. If 1976 was the year of the 'drought tax', it was also the year of the vine, which prefers hot weather to cold and rain. The wines were heavily coloured, tannic, high in alcohol and not at all *primeur*. It was hard to find fruity growths for quick consumption, but the *crus* produced plenty of wine for laying down. This vintage reminded us that if you want to make good Beaujolais – that is to say, fruity, drinkable, light wine – the grapes must not be too ripe; indeed, they must be barely on the threshold of ripeness when they are harvested.

1977: By contrast with 1976, the harvest this year began at the end of September and the wines took a long time to make. Their strong acidity was ill-adapted to *primeur* treatment. The *crus*, however, produced some pleasant surprises and were much in demand on the market.

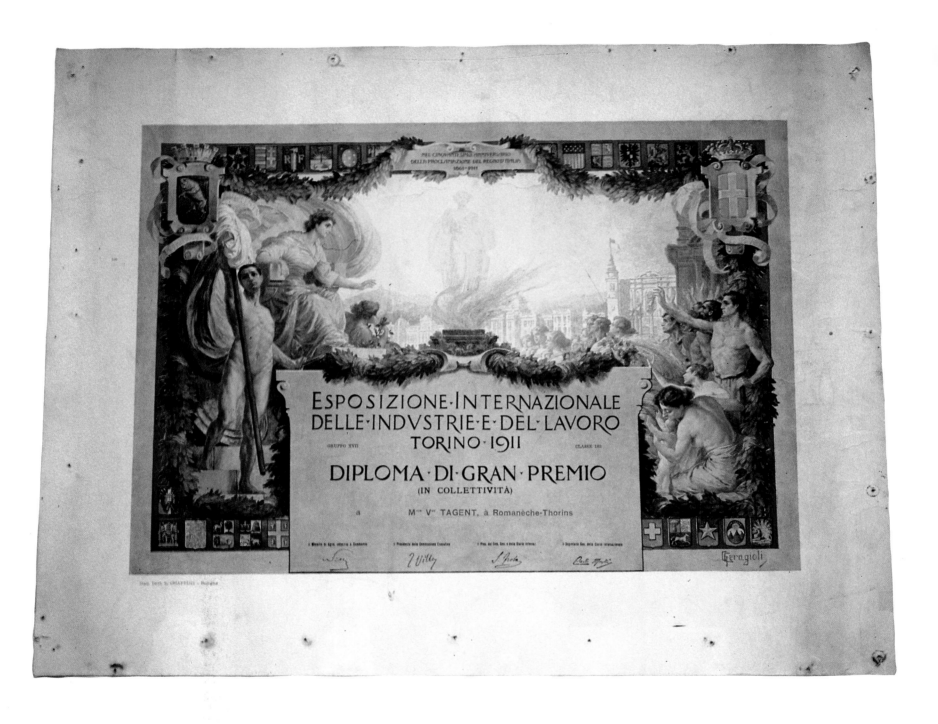

1978: The grapes profited from a spell of sunshine lasting till the end of October, which corrected the effects of an unbalanced summer. After a long time in the making, the wines that emerged after the winter cold had a thoroughly Beaujolais character; which is to say that they were silky and aromatic. Sometimes they had too much of the 'banana' scent (acetate of isoamyl) which characterizes wines made according to the 'whole-grape' method. They proved a commercial success, with the exception of Beaujolais-Villages, which had difficulty adapting to an incoherent tax system that effectively barred them from the restaurant market.

1979: Tender, refined, fruity: such are the most frequent adjectives applied by tasters to the *primeur* wines of the 1979 harvest, the first of year one of obligatory tastings for all AOC

FROM 1800 TO 1900: A CENTURY OF VINTAGES

This extract is from a document compiled by Elisée Portal, a Beaujolais wine-grower, which gives the salient characteristics of each season over a hundred consecutive years. In addition to the quality of the harvests and the current prices, this moving record describes the many plagues that afflicted the Beaujolais during the nineteenth century: pyralis, oidium, phylloxera, frosts . . .

1801: They were valued forty to forty-five francs the cask.
1802: They were valued at eighty francs the cask.
1803: A very hot year, early harvest. Superior quality.
1804: Rainy year, good quality. Abundant quantity.
1805: Rainy year, late harvest, slump in wines, quality detestable.
1806: Frosts. Fifty francs a cask. Good quality.
1807: Heat and drought. Abundant and good quality harvest.
1808: Much rain. Forty-five francs the cask. Abundant harvest, mediocre quality.
1809: The grapes did not ripen. Small harvest.
1810: Hard winter, the vines froze.
1811: Very hot year, wine expensive, excellent, small quantity. The wine of the comet.
1812: The grapes ripened poorly. High quantity, low quality.
1814: Low quality, high quantity, one hundred and ten francs the cask.
1815: Heat waves. One hundred francs the cask.
1816: Terrible year, rainy, cold, one hundred and twenty francs the cask, low quantity, bad quality.
1817: Hail at the end of July. One hundred and fifteen francs the cask. Quality and quantity only average.
1818: Heat, drought, eighty francs the cask. Abundance and quality.
1819: Heat, one hundred francs the cask. Abundance and quality.
1820: Wine sold badly, forty-five francs the cask. Small harvest, bad quality.
1821: Sixty francs the cask.
1822: Heat waves, harvest began August 15, never seen since 1552.
1823: Eighty francs the cask.
1824: Seventy francs the cask.
1825: Spring frosts, hot summer, excellent quality, poor in quantity.
1826: Fifty francs the cask.
1827: Rain, wine prices up. Abundant harvest, poor quality.
1828: Rain, forty francs the cask.
1829: One of the best years of the Restoration, exceptional in both quality and quantity.
1830: Much damaged by pyralis. Small harvest, good quality.
1831: Eighty francs the cask. Vines ugly, small harvest, good quality.
1832: Appearance of the comet which Béranger wrote about. Small harvest, excellent quality.
1833: Heavy drought, prices rising.
1834: Old wines of great growths now worth one hundred and fifty francs the cask. Good harvest, both quality and quantity.
1835: Bad hail at the end of May. Undistinguished harvest from all points of view.
1836: Rain, hail, one hundred francs the cask. Small harvest.
1837: Worms still causing damage.
1838: Heat waves in August. Seventy francs the cask. Small harvest.
1839: Rain, sixty-five francs the cask. Poor harvest.
1840: Partial frosts. Floods at Dracé. Good harvest.
1841: Vines poorly. Slow flowering. Small harvest.
1842: Very hot in July and August. One hundred and twenty francs the cask. Small harvest, good wine.
1843: Pyralis damage. Ninety francs the cask. Mediocre harvest from every point of

1844: Many storms. Seventy francs the cask. Mediocre from all points of view.
1845: Pyralis doing much damage. Very bad harvest.
1846: Heat, drought. Very bad harvest.
1847: Twenty-five francs the cask. Abundant harvest, good quality.
1848: Heavy drought. Chiroubles 11 degrees, abundance and quality.
1849: Romanèche wines, 11 degrees 1.
1850: Heat. Fifty francs the cask. Abundant harvest, variable quality.
1851: Frost in the plain, snow in May. Mediocre harvest.
1852: Vines seem sick: mildew. Very mediocre harvest.
1853: Humid, cold, frost, mildew. Worst year of the century.
1854: Frost. Moulin-à-Vent 12 degrees 8. Small harvest, excellent quality.
1855: Mildew receding. Small harvest, excellent quality.
1856: Rain at flowering. Small harvest.
1857: Drought. Morgon 11 degrees 5.
1858: Comet at harvest time. Heat wave. Middling harvest, good wine.
1859: Fleurie 12 degrees 5, Morgon 11 degrees 9, middling harvest.
1860: Heavy rains, heavy frosts. Poor wines, christened 'Garibaldi'.
1861: Partial freeze on June 9. One hundred francs the cask. Middling harvest.
1862: Slight spring frosts, sixty francs the cask. Middling harvest.
1863: Heat in July and August. Early harvest. Good harvest, superior quality.
1864: Harvest at beginning of September. Seventy francs the cask. Good harvest.
1865: Best year of the period.
1866: Harvested in the rain. Very heavy yield, passable quality.
1867: Frost in the plain on May 27, 28, 29. Poor quality, middling quantity.
1868: Heavy harvest. Difficult sales. Good wines for keeping.
1869: Kept in the vats by wine-growers.
1870: Drought, disastrous hail just before the harvest. Prices up to one hundred and
      fifty francs the cask.
1871: Localized frosts, hard winter. Loss on harvest.
1872: Winter frosts causing much damage. Loss on harvest.
1873: Frost on April 27, plenty of rain. Poor harvest.
1874: Frost in the plain on May 6. Abundant harvest, superior wines.
1875: Year of France's most abundant harvest ever.
1876: Snow at the end of April. Good harvest.
1877: Hail at Brouilly. Ninety francs the cask.
1878: Mildew causing damage. Good harvest.
1880: Terrible winter. The vines froze. One hundred and thirty francs the cask.
1881: Phylloxera. Frost. One hundred and sixty francs the cask.
1882: Frost in April. Disastrous rain in July. Bad harvest.
1883: Rainy summer. Bad harvest.
1884: Frost and hail on April 22. Bad harvest.
1885: Vines being pulled up at a great rate. Bad harvest.
1886: Planting American vines and grafting on to them. Loss on harvest.
1887: One hundred and five francs the cask. Loss on harvest.
1888: Replanting. One hundred and thirty francs the cask. Loss on harvest.
1889: Hail on July 13. Loss on harvest.
1890: Hail on August 2. Loss on harvest.
1891: Hail on June 7. Loss on harvest.
1892: Hail on the plain. One hundred francs the cask. Middling harvest.
1893: Early harvest. Cyclone. Good harvest, good quality.
1894: Ninety francs the cask. Abundant harvest.
1895: Drought. Hailstorms. Middling harvest.
1896: Rot, heavy harvest, bad quality.
1897: Mildew. Seventy-five francs the cask. Middling harvest. Bad quality.
1898: Hot September, ninety-five francs the cask. Middling harvest, quality good.
1899: Localized frosts. Middling harvest. Incomplete quality.
1900: Rot. Nowhere to put the wine, so thrown out. Five to twenty-five francs the cask.

French wines. The *crus* followed well, thanks to their solid construction, sustained colour, satisfactory body and characteristic aromas.

1980: If the 1980 vintage has been generally unmemorable for wine lovers, it will nonetheless leave behind a few good growths, especially among the *crus* harvested at middling altitudes. These were rich in colour, without excessive acidity; clean in the mouth, pure in the nose. They should be drunk soon, being ill-equipped for ageing.

1981: The year was one of great hopes and great disappointments, because of the uncertain weather – frosts, hail, rains – and cryptogramic diseases. In the end, the harvest took place under favourable conditions and the wines of 1981 sustained colour and an often discreet fruitiness which remained harmonious in the mouth. The *crus* turned out full

bodied, powerful (but not too powerful) and with promise of good possibilities for ageing.

1982: The 1982 harvest was one of the heaviest of the last ten years. The wine was typically *primeur*: just what the customers wanted. Supple, fruity, light in colour, with the characteristic 'acid drop' perfume, '82s were not, like '81s, wines for keeping.

1983: By contrast with the 1982 wines (whose constituents were all too often diluted by the abundance of the harvest), '83s are remarkably concentrated. This reduced yields and increased aromatic richness. Their colour is a stunning purplish ruby. The flavour is fruity, with raspberry or redcurrant overtones; the wine has body and generosity and while there were problems encountered in bringing it quickly on to the market it appears certain to keep well.

1984: This vintage was slightly late, but in the end provided classic Beaujolais wines with a record quality of *primeur* – nearly 485,000 hectolitres. The wines of 1984 are well coloured, rich in primary aromas (such as banana and iris) and very drinkable. The *crus* are typical in character, but their constitution is too delicate for them to keep long.

1985: The harvest began around September 20 and was followed by a sunny, hot, dry autumn which severely tested vinification skills. The grapes were perfectly healthy, however, and the resultant wine was generous in colour, with a scent of bananas and violets that developed over a period of months. The *vins de primeur* established a new record with sales exceeding 515,000 hectolitres.

EXPOSITION UNIVERSELLE
LIÉGE 1905
SOUS LE HAUT PATRONAGE DE S.M. LE ROI DES BELGES
SOUS LA PRÉSIDENCE D'HONNEUR DE S.A.R. MONSEIGNEUR LE COMTE DE FLANDRE
ET SOUS LA PRÉSIDENCE DE S.A.R. MONSEIGNEUR LE PRINCE ALBERT DE BELGIQUE

GROUPE X – CLASSE 60
FRANCE

Diplôme de Médaille d'Argent

DÉCERNÉ A MONSIEUR AUDRAS, IVAN.
A JULIÉNAS (RHONE).

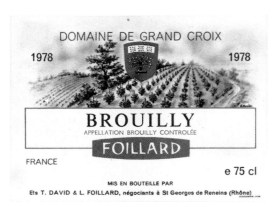

DOMAINE DE GRAND CROIX
1978   1978

BROUILLY
APPELLATION BROUILLY CONTROLÉE
FOILLARD

FRANCE   e 75 cl

MIS EN BOUTEILLE PAR
Ets T. DAVID & L. FOILLARD, négociants à St Georges de Reneins (Rhône)

Mis en bouteille au Domaine

MORGON
Domaine
Princesse Lieven
Appellation Morgon Contrôlée

1978

Produce of France

G.F.A. du Domaine de S.A.S. La Princesse Lieven
Propriétaire-Récoltant à Villié-Morgon (Rhône - France)

75 cl

Chénas
APPELLATION CHÉNAS CONTROLÉE
Vin du Beaujolais

1979   13°

70 cl

CAVE DU CHATEAU DE CHÉNAS
SOCIÉTÉ COOPÉRATIVE VINICOLE A CHÉNAS (Rhône)
Importé par G. THIESSEN-MAASTRICHT Négociants en Vins depuis 1740

LABELS OF THE BEAUJOLAIS

Charles QUITTANSON

DRESSING UP WINE

The label is to the bottle what dress is to a woman. A dress clothes the female form without changing it. It emphasizes her qualities, and creates a silhouette which is neither scandalous nor ludicrous, but beautifying. However, if the woman's figure is mediocre or defective, her clothes can make her look even worse. In the same way, the label on a bottle is meant to please, to make the wine inside attractive.

The label should be neither a book, nor a display. It is a window whose harmony leaves its mark on the product behind it. Thus a fine label on a bad product is a mistake, a bait; in short, counter-productive. The reverse is also true. It isn't the cowl that makes the monk, and the label doesn't make the wine; but it does contribute to the wine's embellishment and the wine must be worthy of it.

THE 'RONDEUR-CARRÉ' OF THE WINE LABEL

A wine that is both supple and candid is often described as having a *rondeur-carré* (literally a square-roundness). The same is true of the label. It should be neither offensive nor dubious. It would be offensive if its design or its tone were in poor taste. And it would be equivocal if its text lacked frankness, or if it were tendentious and misleading.

To read a label is to make the acquaintance of a wine, to want it, to taste it in anticipation. Thus the label should inspire confidence, and 'tame' the potential buyer; for according to Saint Exupéry's *Petit Prince*, to tame something means to create bonds with it. And the fox in the story adds, 'One can only know the things that one has tamed'.

HOW LABELS HAVE CHANGED

The label has many forms. To begin with, it was a simple rectangle, containing an item of information: the name of the merchandise. Exactly like the labels on our grandmothers' pots of jam: Quince 19 . ., Raspberry 19 . .. Then the label was perfected, becoming more descriptive and complimentary. It acquired drawings and illustrations, often coloured ones. Graphic designs changed with the fashions. At the beginning of the century, labels tended to be in the art nouveau style, with complicated curvature like the entrances of the Paris Métro. Modern art followed, and now the vogue is for sober, almost academic work.

Sometimes the label will show a coat of arms, sometimes a landscape, people, a cellar, or a house. In order to avoid any confusion about the wine's name or characteristics, these illustrations must not lead the consumer to believe that the wine has an origin or a quality that it does not possess. A *château*, for example, can only be depicted if the wine comes from a vineyard designated *château* in the sense of 'local, honest and consistent' practices. The label often carries a trade mark. The first ones were charming, like *Au plaisir de ma belle, Le lait des vieillards, Le jus gaulois, Vin d'amour, L'escadron en folie, La santé par les plantes*, or *Délices nocturnes*. These were perilously close to broad jokes. Today, however, wine once again tends to be serious.

The label may be rectangular, oval, lozenge-shaped, or round. It can also form a band placed at an angle across the bottle. It is frequently complemented by a shield or collar on the shoulder of the bottle. On this the vintage is usually inscribed.

Sometimes a pendant is attached to the neck of the bottle. This element usually describes the wine's place of origin and outlines the best way to serve it.

THE LABEL AS A SOURCE OF INFORMATION

The principle of labelling is as follows: everything not authorized by community regulations (whether obligatory or optional) is forbidden.

Château des Gimarets

MOULIN-A-VENT

appellation moulin-à-vent controlée

Mis en bouteille par
LES CAVES DE CHAMPCLOS, Belleville (Rhône) France

Vicomte
Bernard de Romanet
Saint-Jean-d'Ardières F. 69220

1982

FLEURIE

Appellation Fleurie Controlée

Produit de France

Mis en bouteille par F. 6964 à Saint-Jean-d'Ardières
Sélectionné par Vicomte Bernard de Romanet
à Saint-Jean-d'Ardières F. 69220

BEAUJOLAIS-VILLAGES

APPELLATION BEAUJOLAIS-VILLAGES CONTROLÉE

MISE EN BOUTEILLES DANS LA RÉGION DE PRODUCTION PAR

Les Caves de Champclos 750 ml

BELLEVILLE-SUR-SAONE (RHONE) FRANCE

IMP. CLOS DU MOULIN - 01140 THOISSEY

Beaujolais

APPELLATION CONTROLÉE

75 cl

Mis en bouteille par THORIN   F 71570 PONTANEVAUX
Product of France

IMP. CLOS DU MOULIN · 01140 THOISSEY

TRADE MARK

Produce of France

Beaujolais

APPELLATION BEAUJOLAIS CONTRÔLÉE

SÉLECTIONNÉ ET MIS EN BOUTEILLES PAR
PAUL SAPIN VINS FINS A LANCIÉ (RHÔNE) FRANCE

75 cl

PAUL SAPIN

LA SEULE MAISON DE BOURGOGNE
AYANT OBTENU LA
GRANDE MÉDAILLE TRADITION FRANCE

MAISON FONDÉE EN 1865

GRANDS VINS   DE BOURGOGNE

Chiroubles

APPELLATION CHIROUBLES CONTROLÉE

MOMMESSIN

NÉGOCIANT - ÉLEVEUR A MÂCON (S & L) FRANCE

Beaujolais Supérieur

Appellation Beaujolais Supérieur Contrôlée

CHÂTEAU DU GRAND TALANCÉ

Mis en bouteilles au Château pour

J. PELLERIN À SAINT-GEORGES-DE-RENEINS (RHÔNE) FRANCE

75 cl

Château de Nervers
1984

CUVÉE CHOISIE
PAR
PAUL BOCUSE

RESTAURATEUR
A
COLLONGES-AU-MONT-D'OR

Brouilly

APPELLATION BROUILLY CONTROLÉE

MIS EN BOUTEILLE A ROMANECHE-THORINS
PAR LE SAVOUR CLUB, NÉGOCIANT A LANCIÉ, RHÔNE

Savour Club

PRODUCE
OF FRANCE

75 cl

PRODUIT DE FRANCE

 **CHÂTEAU DE BUSSY**

APPELLATION BEAUJOLAIS CONTROLÉE

Beaujolais

mis en bouteille   en région de production

par Joseph VERNAISON   BELLEVILLE 69220 FRANCE   e **75 cl**

TRADITION

Clochemerle

Beaujolais-Villages

APPELLATION BEAUJOLAIS-VILLAGES CONTRÔLÉE

75 cl

Mis en bouteilles en exclusivité par
MAISON FRANÇOIS PAQUET, NÉGOCIANT-ÉLEVEUR, LE PERRÉON (RHÔNE)

FRANCE

IMP. DURAND 71006

PRODUCE OF FRANCE

DEPUIS 1849

LE PIAT DE BEAUJOLAIS

APPELLATION BEAUJOLAIS CONTRÔLÉE

MIS EN BOUTEILLE PAR PIAT PÈRE & FILS

NÉGOCIANTS-ÉLEVEURS A LA CHAPELLE-DE-GUINCHAY, S.-&-L.

FRANCE

750 ml e

Beaujolais-Villages

APPELLATION CONTRÔLÉE

Domaine de la Sorbière

Mis en bouteille au Domaine

75 cl

S.A.R.L. DES DOMAINES **JEAN-CHARLES PIVOT**
"LA ROCHE" QUINCIÉ-EN-BEAUJOLAIS - 69430 BEAUJEU FRANCE

Domaine de la Bourdonnière

MORGON
APPELLATION MORGON CONTROLÉE

MIS EN BOUTEILLES PAR
T. DAVID & L. FOILLARD
NÉGOCIANTS A ST-GEORGES-DE-RENEINS (Rhône)

FRANCE

e 75 cl

L. WITRANT Propriétaire à Lantignié

IMP. CLOS DU MOULIN · 01140 THOISSEY

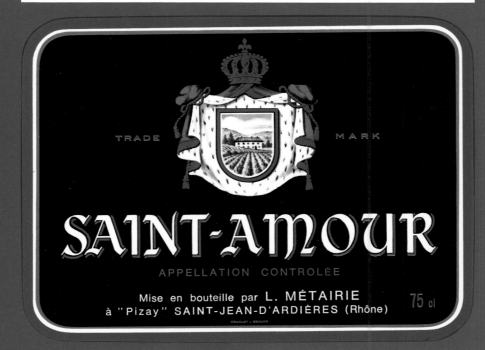

TRADE   MARK

SAINT-AMOUR
APPELLATION CONTROLÉE

Mise en bouteille par L. MÉTAIRIE
à "Pizay" SAINT-JEAN-D'ARDIÈRES (Rhône)

75 cl

PIGUALET · BEAUNE

PRODUCE

OF FRANCE

BROUILLY
APPELLATION BROUILLY CONTRÔLÉE

MIS EN BOUTEILLE PAR AUJOUX, A St-GEORGES-DE-RENEINS (69) FRANCE

PRODUIT DE FRANCE

MOULIN A VENT

APPELLATION MOULIN-A-VENT CONTROLÉE

75 cl

MIS EN BOUTEILLES PAR

CHANUT FRÈRES

Négociant-Eleveur à Romanèche-Thorins (Saône-et-Loire) France

G / 7975 / a

création imp. gougenheim lyon

1984
A BOIRE
FRAIS

appellation beaujolais
contrôlée

MIS EN BOUTEILLE EN BEAUJOLAIS
PAR E. LORON ET FILS
A PONTANEVAUX S.L. (FRANCE)

70 cl

PRODUIT DE FRANCE

CHIROUBLES

APPELLATION   CONTRÔLÉE

750 ml

mis en bouteille par

Jacques Dépagneux négociant à Villefranche (Rhône)

G / 24

création imp. gougenheim lyon

Beaujolais-Villages

DEPUIS 1865

Mis en bouteille et choisi pour vous par

Didier Mommessin

MOMMESSIN

75cl

Les Vins Mommessin à La Grange Saint-Pierre - France 71000

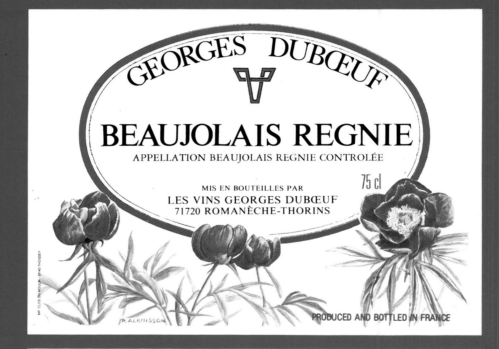

GEORGES DUBŒUF

BEAUJOLAIS REGNIE

APPELLATION BEAUJOLAIS REGNIE CONTROLÉE

MIS EN BOUTEILLES PAR
LES VINS GEORGES DUBŒUF
71720 ROMANÈCHE-THORINS

75 cl

PRODUCED AND BOTTLED IN FRANCE

CHIROUBLES

APPELLATION CHIROUBLES CONTROLÉE

75 cl

MIS EN BOUTEILLE PAR
CLUB FRANÇAIS DU VIN   LANCIÉ 69220 FRANCE

PRODUIT DE FRANCE

DOMAINE BRISSON

APPELLATION MORGON CONTROLÉE

Morgon

mis en bouteille   en région de production

par Joseph-VERNAISON   BELLEVILLE 69220 FRANCE

e 75 cl

L. RUEL POITIERS III

JEAN-MARIE LORON   FONDATEUR EN 1821

Beaujolais Villages

APPELLATION CONTROLÉE

CUVÉE DU FONDATEUR

Product of France   e 75 cl

MIS EN BOUTEILLE PAR E. LORON & FILS - PONTANEVAUX (FRANCE)

"cuvée de la belle vie"

PRODUCE OF FRANCE   75 cl

BEAUJOLAIS-VILLAGES

Appellation Beaujolais-Villages Contrôlée

MIS EN BOUTEILLE A 69820 FLEURIE PAR

QUINSON FILS

IMP CLOS DU MOULIN - 01140 THOISSEY

Mis en bouteilles par

LOUIS TÊTE

St Didier sur Beaujeu, Rhône

Côte de Brouilly

APPELLATION COTE DE BROUILLY CONTROLÉE

70 cl

PRODUCE OF FRANCE

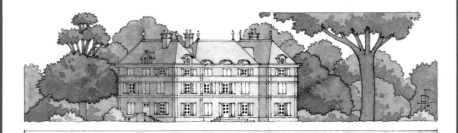

CHATEAU DU PETIT TALANCÉ

BEAUJOLAIS

APPELLATION BEAUJOLAIS CONTROLÉE

MIS EN BOUTEILLES PAR

T. DAVID & L. FOILLARD

FRANCE   NÉGOCIANTS A ST-GEORGES-DE-RENEINS (Rhône)   e 75 cl

Mᴿ CLOS DU MOULIN - 01140 THOISSEY

Jean Lafitte

Produce of France

JULIÉNAS

APPELLATION JULIÉNAS CONTROLÉE

*Je ne connais de sérieux
ici-bas que la culture de
la vigne.* VOLTAIRE

75 cl   Mis en Bouteille par

LES CHAIS RÉUNIS A VILLEFRANCHE-SUR-SAÔNE

MOULIN-A-VENT

APPELLATION MOULIN-A-VENT CONTROLÉE

75 cl

Mis en bouteilles par
Albert DAILLY à Romanèche-Thorins (S.-et-L.)

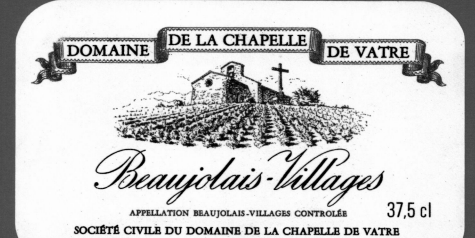

DOMAINE **DE LA CHAPELLE** DE VATRE

Beaujolais-Villages

APPELLATION BEAUJOLAIS-VILLAGES CONTROLÉE

37,5 cl

SOCIÉTÉ CIVILE DU DOMAINE DE LA CHAPELLE DE VATRE

MIS EN BOUTEILLE PAR R. SARRAU, SAINT-JEAN-D'ARDIÈRES, RHONE, FRANCE

LA JACQUIÈRE

PRODUCE OF FRANCE

®

BEAUJOLAIS

Appellation Beaujolais Contrôlée

Mis en bouteille par

AUJOUX

750 ml

À SAINT-GEORGES DE RENEINS (RHONE)

CHÂTEAU DE JAVERNAND

CHIROUBLES

APPELLATION CHIROUBLES CONTRÔLÉE

Sélectionné et mis en bouteilles par

GEORGES DUBŒUF NÉGOCIANT A 71720 ROMANÈCHE-THORINS, FRANCE

PRODUCE OF FRANCE

37,5 cl

PRODUCT OF FRANCE

1983

Romanorum Villa in Agro Thorinse (IXᵉ Siècle)

CHATEAU DES JACQUES

Moulin-à-Vent

APPELLATION MOULIN-A-VENT CONTROLÉE

75 cl

SOCIÉTÉ CIVILE D'EXPLOITATION DE ROMANÈCHE-THORINS

PROPRIÉTAIRES-RÉCOLTANTS 71570 LA CHAPELLE-DE-GUINCHAY

PRODUIT FRANÇAIS

BROUILLY

APPELLATION BROUILLY CONTROLEE

Domaine de la Folie

Mis en bouteille par J. BEDIN à 69830 BLACERET - FRANCE

RED TABLE WINE ALC. 12,5 % BY VOL. PRODUCT OF FRANCE CONT. : 750 ML

Imported by : *Franche Comté*, Ltd., FAIR LAWN, N.J.

Moulin à Vent

DOMAINE DE CHAMP DE COUR
APPELLATION MOULIN-A-VENT CONTROLEE

MOMMESSIN

Négociant à la Grange Saint-Pierre, 71000 France

ANNE ᴅᴇ BEAUJEU

BEAUJOLAIS·VILLAGES
APPELLATION BEAUJOLAIS-VILLAGES CONTROLÉE

750 ml   1984

Mis en bouteille par
THOMAS LA CHEVALIÈRE
NÉGOCIANT A BEAUJEU (FRANCE)   № 14007
Produce of France

"LA ROILETTE"

FLEURIE
APPELLATION FLEURIE CONTROLÉE

MIS EN BOUTEILLE PAR
VINS DESSALLE
69220 SAINT-JEAN-D'ARDIÈRES (RHONE) FRANCE

Red Burgundy Wine	selected & imported by	Contents 750 ml
	Grape Expectations	
Produce of France	emeryville, california	Alcohol 13% Vol.

GEORGES DUBŒUF

BEAUJOLAIS-VILLAGES

APPELLATION BEAUJOLAIS-VILLAGES CONTROLÉE

MIS EN BOUTEILLES PAR

75 cl

LES VINS GEORGES DUBŒUF
71720 ROMANECHE - THORINS

PRODUCED AND BOTTLED IN FRANCE

BON VIN NE PEUT MENTIR

R.S

TIRAGE
DE PRIMEUR

TIRAGE
DE PRIMEUR

BEAUJOLAIS~VILLAGES NOUVEAU

APPELLATION BEAUJOLAIS-VILLAGES CONTROLÉE

Robert Sarrau

70 cl

Mis en bouteille par R. Sarrau à St Jean d'Ardières - France

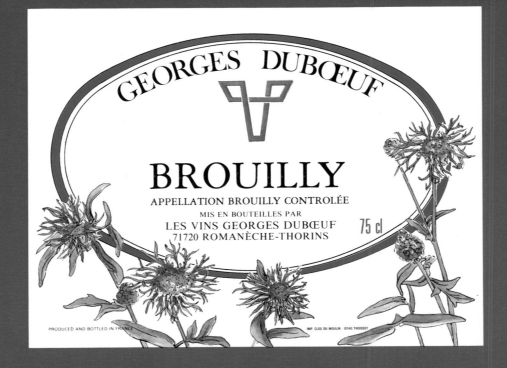

GEORGES DUBŒUF

BROUILLY

APPELLATION BROUILLY CONTROLÉE

MIS EN BOUTEILLES PAR

LES VINS GEORGES DUBŒUF
71720 ROMANÈCHE-THORINS

75 cl

PRODUCED AND BOTTLED IN FRANCE

Produce of France

LA DYNASTIE DES FERRAUD
1882-1982

De Vigne... en Verre

Moulin-à-Vent

150 cl   APPELLATION CONTRÔLÉE

Elevé et mis en bouteilles par Pierre FERRAUD 69220 Belleville (France)

Moulin à Vent
DES Hospices

APPELLATION MOULIN-A-VENT CONTROLÉE

Authentique, mis en Bouteilles sous le
Contrôle de la Commission administrative
des Hospices

Le Président Fondateur :   par le Concessionnaire Général
                                  BOURISSET S.A.R.L.
75 cl   à CRÈCHES (Saône-et-Loire)

Récolte des Hospices Civils de Romanèche Thorins (France)

CHATEAU DE LONGSARD

BEAUJOLAIS
APPELLATION BEAUJOLAIS CONTROLÉE

MIS EN BOUTEILLES PAR LES PRODUCTEURS RÉUNIS

CELLIER DES SAMSONS   e 70 cl
"LE PONT DES SAMSONS" QUINCIÉ-EN-BEAUJOLAIS (RHONE)

PRODUCE OF FRANCE

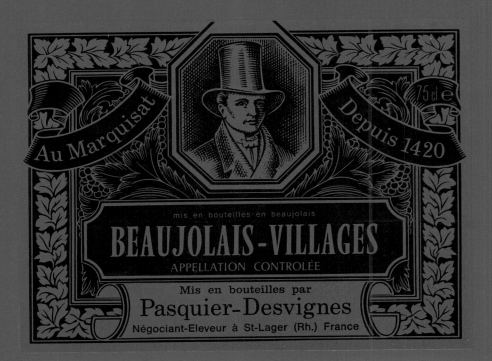

mis en bouteilles en beaujolais

BEAUJOLAIS-VILLAGES

APPELLATION CONTROLÉE

Mis en bouteilles par

Pasquier-Desvignes

Négociant-Eleveur à St-Lager (Rh.) France

Au Marquisat · Depuis 1420 · 75 cl

PRODUCE OF FRANCE

MAISON FONDÉE
EN 1844

FLEURIE

APPELLATION FLEURIE CONTROLÉE

Pommier Frères

Mis en bouteille par

POMMIER FRÈRES NÉGOCIANTS-ÉLEVEURS

A VILLEFRANCHE-SUR-SAÔNE - RHÔNE - FRANCE   75 cl

G / 4644 / a   CRÉATION IMP. GOUGENHEIM, LYON

vignobles · de France

Récolte   1984

MOULIN-A-VENT

APPELLATION MOULIN-A-VENT CONTROLÉE   75 cl

Mis en bouteilles par

Pasquier Desvignes

au Marquisat, Négociants à St-Lager (Rh.) France

The rule established by the law of France, which recognizes that any declarations can be used which are not expressly forbidden, no longer applies when the presentation and designation of wines are at issue. Information the label has to give:
– The denomination, with a distinction between *vins de table*, *vins de pays* and imported wines.
– The nominal volume; that is, the volume of liquid in the bottle.
– The name (or trade name); and the quality and address of the bottler or packer.
– The name of the country of production.

OPTIONAL INFORMATION (APPLICABLE TO BEAUJOLAIS WINES)

– Wine colour
– Alcometric level
– Production mode (such as *vin nouveau, vin primeur* . . .)
– Year of harvest
– Traditional indications (for example, *clos* . . .)
– The place name completing the *appellation d'origine* (such as Fleurie 'Grille-Midi'; Brouilly 'Pisse-Vieille')
– A commercial, factory or service trade mark
– The names and addresses of those who have taken part in the commercializing of the wine (for example, for a wine-merchant's wine, the name of the wine-grower)
– The name of the vineyard (for example, Château des Gimarets, Domaine de Couroy . . .)
– Any indication relative to bottling (for example, *mise en bouteille à la propriété*)
– The prize, or prizes, officially bestowed on the wine in question (for example, *Médaille d'Or du Concours Général Agricole, Grumage de l'Ordre des Compagnons du Beaujolais*)
– Advice to consumers (such as *servir frais*)
– The number of the bottle.

LE VIN DE LA JOIE

Michel AULAS

Beaujolais is the work of the earth, of vines, of the weather . . . and of wine-growers.

The wine-grower plants his vines, then cares for them all year round. He brings them manure and fertilizer; prunes them carefully; treats them against diseases; defends them against insects and worms; and then, if they have been spared by hail and frost, harvests his grapes.

And then the wine-grower makes his wine, often following the advice of highly qualified technicians; oenologists, who are chemists, pharmacists, savants and artists – in short, magicians. Oenologists are more and more numerous nowadays and more and more in demand. They are the doctors who deliver the grape at the birth of *vin nouveau*, and the guides of the living liquid when it is still in its early youth. They know how to direct whole orchestras of organoleptic elements and subtle aldehydes, till they reach a crescendo of sweetness. Lastly, they are the physicians of the wine as it continues to 'sing in the bottle'.

In the Beaujolais, the oenologist's task is to produce and raise, side by side with the wine-growers and then with the wine-merchants, a wine that is 'sweet as a memory ripened by hope'. This is the *vin de la joie* of the Beaujolais. For of all the compliments bestowed on it by its lovers, the most sincere is that this is a truly happy wine.

BEAUJOLAIS AS IT IS DESCRIBED

If a book were made to contain the names of the world's great men who have visited the Beaujolais, and admired its landscapes, its people and its wines, that book would rapidly assume the proportions of the *Almanach de Gotha* – especially if their comments were included.

Pierre Perret, passing through La Grange-Charreton, was given the Pisse-Vieille of the Hospices de Beaujeu to try. He drank deep, then raised his face to exclaim: 'If every old woman in the world pissed like that, I'd have a hospice all of my own!'

The British Consul-General at Lyon, Sir Paar, a shrewd judge of Beaujolais, was once heard to say (apropos of a Fleurie):

'When one drinks Beaujolais, one wishes one had a neck as long as a swan's, to make the pleasure last longer.'

Edouard Herriot commented:

'In the scent of Beaujolais, is there not that "something of wingèd lightness" which according to Plato is the essence of poetry?'

And the Belgian writer, Jean Lurkin, proclaimed that:

'The real France is rarely to be found on the Faubourg Montmartre, but always between Villefranche and Beaujeu.'

A circumspect tasting

Fête at Clochemerle
(Vaux-en-Beaujolais)

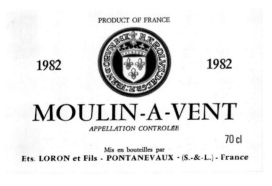

For the rest, I was lucky enough to meet Colette in 1947 at the house of Madeleine and Jean Guillemet at Limas, near Villefranche. This great lady, already ill but nonetheless seduced by the Beaujolais, wrote the following lines on returning from a pilgrimage to a winery:

'What could I expect of the Beaujolais wine-harvest? The endless torrid heat, my own impotence, everything conspired to keep me away from such an arduous occasion. I should have been content with the sounds of the grape-gathering in the hills, the creaking of the waggons as they passed along the little road by which I slept my morning sleep. The voices, thick with dawn fatigue, began at the top of the neighbouring vineyards, then moved downward, downward as the sun rose higher. I visualized the slow harvest, the full baskets, the thirst which one thinks can be slaked by eating grapes, but which the grapes make worse . . .

'Yet I had more than this. Friendship can accomplish much. A chain of kindly arms one day bore me down to the car and I encountered the wine in the secrecy of one of its intimate chambers, whose threshold I never dreamed I would cross.

'In the cool breast of the hill, the wine received me, and not once did I have to put my foot to the ground. In my chariot, I felt like a conqueror . . . the great doors swung inward; the wine seemed to be withdrawn far back in a grotto, and from its high ceiling it flung down an icy blast of still air, the divine and muddy odour of pressed grapes and their bubbling ferment. A hundred metres of vaulting stretched beyond me, twinkling with lamps. Long pink trails of foam ran down the sides of the vats; a team of dappled horses, bluish in the half-light, nonchalantly munched on fallen grape-clusters; the spirit of the young wine, heavy, new-born, impure, blended with the vapour rising from the sweating horses . . .'

Louis Orizet, after a lengthy contemplation of the colour, *robe*, of a Beaujolais, remarked that it had the colour of 'the thigh of a flustered nymph', and defined it as 'matter progressing toward mind'. Léon Foillard saw Beaujolais as the surest defence against thirst: 'A dreadful affliction which strikes all living creatures, even vegetables, and can lead to death . . . an affliction which can be even more dangerous than it is insidious. For while it is easy to pick out a man who has drunk too much, most of the time it is impossible to guess that a man is suffering from thirst . . .'

The sculptor Michel Lapandery, after trying a red wine from Brouilly, shook his glass and murmured thoughtfully: 'Wine like that is as tender as the skin of a child . . .' Utrillo, the Montmartre painter living at the Château de Saint-Bernard on the far side of the Saône, used to come down to Villefranche regularly for a glass of Beaujolais at the Café de Paris, on the pretext of buying tubes of paint at Jean Guillermet's store. For up at St Bernard, his mother Suzanne Valladon had a habit of watering down Maurice's jugs. After his stay in the Saône valley, Utrillo received the Legion of Honour obtained for him

Pots *of Beaujolais at the station at Lyon*

LA BEAUJOLAISE

Il est en France de doux coteaux,
Où, alignés, vont à l'assaut,
Vrilles au vent, les ceps tordus
Qui sont, au travail, entendus
A puiser au fond de la terre
Du rocher le suc salutaire,
Où l'eau va toute à la rivière,
Où le vin seul emplit les verres.

Aimons le Beaujolais joli
Où la vigne a trouvé son lit,
Aimons le joli Beaujolais
Dont les caves sont les palais.

Il est en France un peuple insigne
Qui a pour maîtresse la vigne;
Son cœur, comme ses pousses, est vert.
Il est rouge, tel son proche hiver,
Aux belles il donne la réplique
Et son âme à la République.
Dur au travail, tendre à l'amie,
D'un pot il régale sa mie.

Chantons le Beaujolais joli,
Tra la li, tra la la, la li
Chantons le joli Beaujolais
Au nom frais comme un ruisselet.

Il est en France un vin fameux
Quand il glisse aux gosiers heureux,
Les yeux reflètent sa malice.
Qu'on se garde bien qu'il vieillisse !
En lui du jour est la chaleur
Et, des belles nuits, la fraîcheur.
A qui le boit tout est aisé,
Il est aux lèvres un long baiser.

Buvons le Beaujolais joli
Qu'il gonfle nos ventres sans pli.
Buvons le joli Beaujolais
Qui nous fait tendre le... mollet.

O Beaujolais, mon bon terroir
Tu es le ciel, sans contredit,
Car, chaque année, de tes pressoirs,
Coule pour tous le paradis.
Aussi aimons, chantons, buvons
Le Beaujolais. Pour lui vivons,
Amis ! heureux de ses bienfaits,
Unis dans un accord parfait.

CHANSON COMPOSÉE PAR CATHERIN BUGNARD
EXTRAIT DE L'*ALMANACH DU BEAUJOLAIS,* 1937

by the good offices of President Herriot – but he never did even a drawing of the sluggish Saône. 'I can't do water', he would say to excuse himself; perhaps he was taking an unconscious revenge for the diluting of his Beaujolais. . . .

LE BEAUJOLAIS NOUVEAU EST ARRIVÉ

Beaujolais is the wine of unaffected pleasure; the ultimate party wine. Everyone who has studied it and tried to discover the personality has agreed on one thing: that Beaujolais should be drunk in bumpers, like the joyous thing it is. Also it must be served cool, in glasses filled to the brim – *rouge-bords*, as Boileau-Despreaux has called them, which became *culs-blancs* in a single draught. For years now, from that moment on November 15 when (according to the law which regulates everything, even our hunger and thirst) the Beaujolais of the year can finally be poured into glasses; on that day a party begins which transcends all frontiers. On November 15, all over the world, a cry of delight is heard: *Le Beaujolais Nouveau est arrivé.*

Hundreds of thousands of hectolitres specially vinified for Beaujolais Primeur, leave the region within a few hours on trucks, trains, ships and planes, bound for the five continents of the earth. Beaujolais Nouveau has been brought to Paris by runners and by balloon . . . many of its admirers come to fetch it on the spot and on the night of November 15, the Beaujolais becomes a kind of vinous Babel, in which all tongues blend into an *esperanto* of new wine. Just before Christmas, the news appears in the form of handbills or scrawled in whitewash on bistro windows – a hymn to joy, a challenge to winter. *Le Beaujolais Nouveau est arrivé*, and to hell with the freezing weather. The wine carries the memory of spring smiles and summers gold . . . Thereafter, from Tokyo to Montreal, by way of Sydney, London, and the twin towers of Notre Dame, the consumption of Beaujolais begins in earnest.

There are the straight drinkers, who reminisce about old time bistros, where friends went to lay plans for

changing the world, and to sit around tables covered in red circles from the bottles. There are the couples who go to pledge their love in the same glass of Beaujolais. There are the connoisseurs, who sample the wine as one might tickle a pretty girl, to feel the silkiness of her skin and sense the freshness of her laughter.

And there is that whole crowd of lookers on, gourmands, and seekers of good fellowship, who came up to the red troughs as if they were paying a visit to a well-loved friend, because he is always there to make skies less grey, neighbours more pleasant, wives more bearable, and work less hard. With this extra advantage – according to the old Beaujolais saying – that the wine drunk by men will later do good to women.

THE BENEFITS OF BEAUJOLAIS

Beaujolais is a gift of God to gatherings of friends, to summer evenings spent playing *boules*, or to family reunions. It is no accident that the first official rules and the first written codification of the game of *boules à la Lyonnaise* were worked out in the Beaujolais by Pierre Guillermet.

The priests of the region use the local wine at communion, when it is transmitted by the Eucharist into the blood of Christ. But they also see it as a philtre of smiling wisdom in this region of small wine-growers, where the oldest and most solid virtues still survive: work, patience, generosity, dignity and love of the job well done.

This *'Civilisation Beaujolaise'* is manifested by a certain way of looking at life and adapting to it, without slavish conformism, and

Moulin-à-Vent, *1923. Utrillo's gift to his godson (private collection)*

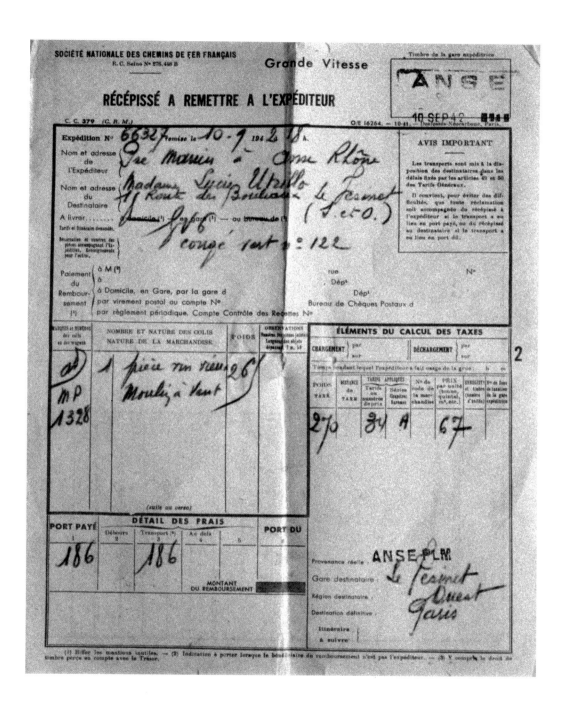

BEAUJOLAIS

Appellation Contrôlée

Cuvée sélectionnée pour Pierre GARAT
par la Jeune Chambre Économique de Belleville

Fleurie

APPELLATION FLEURIE CONTROLÉE

73 cl

DOMAINE DES GRANDES COTES

Stéphane BESSONE
Propriétaire-Récoltant à VAUXRENARD (Rhône)

MIS EN BOUTEILLE A LA PROPRIÉTÉ

St-Didier-sur-Beaujeu, le 14 février 1983

CUVÉE
LANCEMENT

PEUGEOT 205

BEAUJOLAIS-VILLAGES
APPELLATION CONTROLÉE

Cuvée
Spéciale

Tour
de France

BEAUJOLAIS

APPELLATION BEAUJOLAIS CONTROLÉE

0,75 l

UNION INTERPROFESSIONNELLE DES VINS DU BEAUJOLAIS
VILLEFRANCHE (RHONE) FRANCE

BEAUJOLAIS

APPELLATION CONTROLÉE

COMTE B. DE LAGUICHE

PROPRIÉTAIRE A LACHASSAGNE, RHONE

In Boules Lyonnaises, *a very popular game in the Beaujolais, whoever scores no points at all has to kiss 'Fanny' (private collection)*

LA CHANSON DU BEAUJOLAIS

Entre la Cévenne et les Dombes,
Ceinturé d'un ruban d'argent,
Le Beaujolais joyeux s'étend
Avec ses monts avec ses combes.
Au printemps, sous les rayons d'or,
Ses pommiers blancs, ses pêchers roses
Égayent la vigne morose
Qui, paresseuse, dort encor.

Refrain

Oh ! mon joli Beaujolais
Aux sapins verts, aux vignes blondes,
Tes deux aspects je les connais
Les aimant plus que tout au monde.
Sol riche aux flancs généreux,
Ton vin verse l'espérance.
Je te nomme sous ton ciel bleu,
L'un des plus beaux joyaux de France.

II

Dans le temps de la Préhistoire,
Pays tout couvert de forêts
Les fayettes, les loups furets
Se cachaient dans tes combes noires.
Puis, les Romains t'envahissant,
Sur tes flancs, plantèrent la vigne.
Notre sol s'en montra très digne
Et ton bon vin, c'est notre sang.

(Au Refrain)

III

Fait de bons raisins sans mélange,
Ton joli vin c'est un rubis
Rempli des refrains que l'on dit
Au cuvier, les soirs de vendange.
Du vigneron, c'est la fierté.
Du doux poète, c'est la muse.
Mais ce nectar est plein de ruse
Buvons-le sans témérité.

(Au Refrain)

IV

Chère terre toujours féconde
Garde la paix pour ton bonheur.
Reste digne de ton labeur
Ton vin réconfortant le monde.
Il nous faut de robustes bras
Des cœurs vaillants, des âmes fortes
Et sur le seuil de bien des portes,
Je vois encor de nobles gâs.

(Au Refrain)

*Song composed by Zulma Cinquin-Sapin (extract
from* L'Almanach du Beaujolais, *1955)*

without taking things too seriously. Add to this a strong dose of horse sense, gaiety, love of broad jokes, a touch of emotion, earthiness, and the gift of serenity without fatalism.

Take the example of the curate invited to the wedding feast of two of his flock, whose union he had consecrated. With each fresh course that was laid on the table, he raised his glass and exclaimed:

'My Children, with this gift of God, we must drink good Beaujolais wine.' When the dessert arrived, a guest from the City thought it witty to enquire: 'But tell us father, according to you with what should we *not* drink Beaujolais?'
'With water', replied the good curate emptying his glass.

Another story is that of Toine, a small wine-grower who had a wife, Claudine, two goats, a cow, and some chickens. In addition Toine held the post of rural policeman, *garde champêtre*. One day his wife, Claudine, heard him cursing like a trooper down in the stable.
'Toine, whatever's the matter?'
'It's the cow. She won't drink a drop.'
'Well, put your cap on her head. She'll drink all right – more than she can hold.'

And then there is the old Beaujolais saying: 'A woman is like an enema – easier to take than to hold.'

Finally, we would cite the intense

satisfaction derived by the wine-grower from drinking his own wine in his own cool cellar, with its stone pillars and damp sand along the corridors between the lines of barrels – those great casks of 216 litres, each waiting silently for its day.

Though it is a happy wine, Beaujolais also has a way of bringing in a solemn note; for it raises happiness almost to the level of ritual. This is partly the work of the brotherhoods of the Beaujolais, *confréries*. During the course of *Chapitres* or *Tenues*, the *confréries* of the Beaujolais regularly elect new members (provided they have passed certain initiatory tests) from the ranks of neophytes who have been captivated by the juice of the Beaujolais grape.

LES COMPAGNONS DU BEAUJOLAIS

The first of these brotherhoods, and the mother of all of them, is the Confréries des Compagnons du Beaujolais, created soon after the last war, in 1949.

The Fellows, *Compagnons*, are administered by a committee, headed at present by M de Rambuteau. They are in no sense an organization dedicated to folklore, although the members of the committee appear at the various enthronement ceremonies dressed in traditional costumes; that is, round felt hats, green canvas aprons, and black jackets. At their

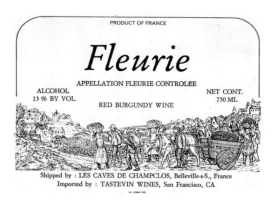

PAVILLON DE L'ÉLYSÉE

EX - LANGER

Jardins des Champs-Elysées

ANJOU 29-60 & 85-10
PARIS VIII⁵

four gatherings, *Tenues* (one per season), they oblige candidates for the brotherhood to drink from giant goblets, *tastevins*, whose content is symbolic; after which they are dubbed on the shoulder with a vine branch, and a silver *tasse* (wine-tasting cup) is hung round their necks by a green cord. Then the candidate is presented with his diploma and signs a register.

But the goals pursued by the *Compagnons* go far beyond their motto – *Vuydons les Tonnaux* (let us drain the barrels). The oath sworn by each new *compagnon* before he goes up to the altar, under the impassive gaze of a wooden Saint-Vincent, is this:

'I swear before Saint-Vincent to behave as a faithful and free *Compagnon de Beaujolais* and to practise the virtues of such. My duty is to love our country, to work to uphold its traditions of hospitality, wisdom and good humour. To make known the beauty of its beautiful places, and the interest of its old churches and ancient *châteaux*, which bear witness to a past enriched by the spirit of its artists and builders. To appreciate and to disseminate the produce of our vines. Lastly, to honour the rugged wine-growers who, by their good work, have forged the prosperity and the reward of our Beaujolais homeland. . . .'

At each enthronement, and in the presence of their 500 guests, the *compagnons* invariably link their association with the great historical tradition of *Compagnonnage*; namely, *savour-faire*, solidarity and fraternity. The wine of the Beaujolais, whose eleven *appellations* take turns presiding over enthronements and reunions, does the rest – which is to say, it spreads a spirit of optimism,

generosity and satisfaction. Thus the revelation experienced by Edouard Herriot one evening at his office on the Quai d'Orsay becomes fact:

'Men have long searched for the original site of Earthly paradise. Scholars, seek no more. Beyond all shadow of doubt, the Garden of Adam and Eve lay close to Quincié, between the valley and the hillcrest. And it was no apple that tempted the first woman. It was a grape. How willingly I pardon her, and how well I understand.'

The *Compagnons du Beaujolais* are to some extent the prophets of that paradise. Since one cannot carry away one's homeland, far less a paradise, on the soles of one's shoes, some of the *Compagnons* have created subsidiaries, known in their language as *devoirs*. Thus there is a *devoir* in Paris. Its members perpetuate the glorious days of the first free French combatants in London. Jean Oberle liked to relate how, during the terrible winter of 1940–41, the first Frenchmen who joined Général de Gaulle sometimes sank into the deepest melancholy. They would try to raise one another's spirits with remarks like: 'The Beaujolais was really admirable at La Mascotte, on Rue des Abbesses' . . . 'I beg your pardon, it was better Chez Ducottier, in the Halle aux Vins'. There is also a Mediterranean *devoir*, one of whose

centres is the Hôtel de la Tour, at Sanary; a Swiss *devoir*, which makes nonsense of the pejorative French expression 'to drink like a Swiss', and others more or less throughout the world: in Germany, England, Belgium, the USA and Canada. Their members are citizens of two nations; one is that of their ancestors – and the other, which they have imbibed, is the Beaujolais.

THE PRAYER OF THE COMPAGNONS

One evening in January 1949, at the Château de Pizay, the *Compagnons du Beaujolais* assembled (both believers and disbelievers) to hear Jean Guillermet read the prayer written for them by the Abbé Pradel. This prayer was inspired by a blend of early Christian visions, the Bible, and the Song of Songs; delivered in the wild accents of Péguy and with true Bacchic ardour, it offers a clear definition of what the *Confrérie des Compagnons* is all about. Their primary concern is to defend and promote the area, *Terroir*, its landscapes, its vineyards, and its people. In this there is an almost religious implication.

'It is very meet, right, and our bounden duty, that we should at all times and places give thanks unto thee Holy Lord, Father Almighty, Eternal God . . .

'But on this day of great and joyous festivity, we give thee thanks that, according to thy will, the sun hath formed upon the hillsides through which the children of men may hold captive unto themselves all the overflowings of its glory . . .

'To the Holy Tree of the vine hast thou given power and lordship over the rays of the daystar, to receive them and blend them with her sap, that we may gather with our hands and drink with our lips the precious and fleeting warmth of the sun . . .

'We give thanks to Thee, O Lord, for all the warmth enclosed in the cool of our cellars.

'We give thanks to Thee, O Lord, for that thy prophets have written that thou wast beloved of a wife, and that thy wife was a vine (. . .)

'We give thanks to Thee, O Lord, for the golden vine which rose up before the gates of thy holy Temple in Jerusalem, in the guise of thy holy nation, as a wife in supplication before her husband . . .

'For by thy union, O Lord, all the vines of the world have been blessed.

'We give thee thanks, O Lord, that to announce the great change desired by all men, thy son did turn six vessels of water into generous wine . . . and that He did choose this fruit of the vine to pour into our innermost being the Blood of his triumphant and living Cross.

'O Lord, we give thee thanks for all the grapes that die for the greater joy and strength of mankind, and for the joy of those who drink . . .

'And for the Mystery of thy Christ, who died for the lives of many and who spoke of the new wine that His disciples would drink in the Kingdom of Heaven . . . and who spoke of new wine each time He announced the coming of the Kingdom of Heaven . . . and again spoke of it on the last night . . .

'And we ask thy blessing, O Lord, on the sun-drenched earth all covered in green vines, which also is blessed by Our Lady in her Chapel of Brouilly, the mother of a Messiah who said these words to His friends gathered for the last supper:

'I am the true vine, and my father is the husbandman. . . .'

MOUNT SINAI IN THE BEAUJOLAIS

One Saturday, around four in the afternoon, some walkers who had climbed the slopes of a mountain covered in vines, were surprised to discover about sixty fellows seated around a table at the top. They wielded their forks with gusto and washed down cold sausages and ham with long draughts of red wine, which must have been delicious, if their prodigious consumption was anything to go by.

This happened at Brouilly, one of the greatest feathers in the cap of the Beaujolais. If you climb this mountain, you will witness a panorama which is among the loveliest in France, a country by no means ill-endowed with views.

The sixty men had climbed Mont Brouilly for a solemn ceremony in honour of the wine of the Beaujolais. I had been summoned by invitation, and as a good citizen of Lyon, familiar since my youth with fine wines, I was able to give a reasonable account of myself in this assembled company.

When we had reached the cheese, a speech was made which ended thus:

'The people from the Ain — we're sorry they're not here. But we are cordially grateful to our Mâconnais guests for coming: and we consider their presence a compliment to our hills. As for all these men of the Beaujolais I see around me, what can I say? They all know us inside out, since there isn't one, I think, with whom I haven't emptied many a bottle. And if there is, let him stand up, and I will instantly give him satisfaction, though I may lie snoring on the field as a result.'

This personation was greeted with roars of approval by the company, who knew the mystique that had inspired it . . . united by countless local bonds, they made up a fine assortment of Beaujolais types. But clouds were threatening to

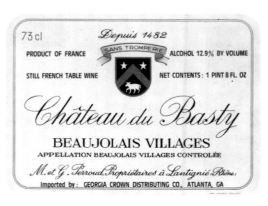

cast a premature pall over the day, and it seemed already as if the light was wavering, as indeed was the landscape before the eyes of my fellow-pilgrims. At this moment a voice, seeming to come from the mists, was heard by the faithful as they waited on their Sinai:

'Go forth and speak in my name. Go forth and graft. Go forth and drink toasts. Go forth, and by the virtues of my wine, fortify those who are weak, warm those who are cold, cheer those who are sad, console those who are in misery, and bring love, concord and joy wherever you go. Go forth and recruit. And each year I shall come back among you and find you more numerous.'

Was the voice human or divine? I shall never know, because most of us were lost in a vague joy of fervent ecstasy. But one real miracle did occur: not one of the worshippers who had climbed that hill a few hours earlier came down it on the seat of his trousers. A proof that Bacchus takes care of the people of the Beaujolais. A proof that he keeps a helping hand on their coat tails, when the road is not straight, and has given them good wives with good sense, who know how to say merely: t'as encore bu un coup, mon homme? *(had another drink, my man?) – without making it an affair of state or grounds for divorce.*

It must be said that the people of this place don't have bad wine, because Beaujolais is a damn good wine which never did anyone any harm. The more you drink of it, the kinder seems your wife, the more faithful your friends, the rosier your future and the more bearable humanity. All the evil in the world is because of one fact: there is only one Beaujolais on the face of the planet. It is here that the elect may be found (and they are few in number, as we know).

GABRIEL CHEVALLIER
EXTRAIT DE *BROUILLY*, DE JUSTIN DUTRAIVE, 1979

169

'GOSIERS SECS' *AND* 'GRAPILLEURS'

The Beaujolais owes much to two other *Confréries*: the *Gosiers Secs de Clochemerle* (the dry-gullets of Clochemerle) and the *Grapilleurs des Pierres Dorées* (gleaners of the Pierres Dorées).

These two associations both seek to set up a *terroir* within a *terroir*. Though united as a body, the Beaujolais is actually made up of a series of tiny areas of climates, *Climats*, and the many *appellations* are justified in many nuances of taste. But this diversity is also perceptible in the countryside and in the people's outlook.

The southern Beaujolais, within a triangle which broadly covers the area between Villefranche, Lamure and L'Arbresle, has a strong originality of its own. This derives, first of all, from the stone, which is the colour of good fresh bread; all the villages are built of it, and the chequerboard of vineyards, divided by drystone walls, has its tint. The gentle inclines of the valleys give this country of ochre sandstone a special beauty. Here are woodlands as well as vines, which add an element of silence and intimacy. There are also plenty of *Garrigues*, areas of rough vegetation, which are used for raising goats for the production of a cheese which goes well with the local wine. Mushrooms gathered in the woods add a distinctive flavour to the local dishes of *civet au capucin* (jugged hare) or *coq au vin*.

The yellow houses with their Roman tiles, the churches, the *châteaux*, the wayside crosses and the *cadoles*, those doll's houses one sees at the corners of the vineyards, all combine to produce a landscape reflecting the patience and hard work of the men who live in it. Even its legends of haunted dungeons, dark forests and gloomy crypts have the air of fireside confidences. Most of all perhaps, the originality of the *Pays des Pierres Dorées* lies in its balance of custom, scenery and history. It is a kind of Beaujolais *Touraine*, a place that knows how to live well.

The latter science – innate of course – is what the *Grapilleurs des*

MENU

Le Consommé Souveraine

Les Truites du Rhône en Bellevué
Sauce Tartare

Les Chevalières de Poulardes à l'Amiral

Les Fonds d'Artichauts Païva

Les Faisans Rôtis sur Canapés

La Salade Ninon

Les Glaces Antinéa

Les Corbeilles de Fruits

Les Desserts

VINS DE LA RÉGION

Morgon en Carafes

Viré en Carafes

Condrieu Viognier de Pays 1927

Moulin à Vent 1923

Ch. Heidsieck Dry Frappé

Lyon, le 7 Janvier 1934

BERRIER ET MILLIET

E.R. CUZENT

20^e

Anniversaire de la « Grappe Fleurie »

Menu

La Terrine du Chef

Le Gratin de Fruits de Mer

Le Rôti de Porc aux Pruneaux

Les Fromages

La Tarte aux Pommes

▽

Vin de Fleurie

△

MAISON DES BEAUJOLAIS
Le Samedi 2 Janvier 1971

Attends, mon Vieux !

Quand j'y descends, je marche droit.
De mon vieux vin, je bois un doigt,

Un doigt, deux doigts et je me grise
A moi le mur, le pilier ?
Je ne trouve plus l'escalier.

"All right, all right, you've convinced us — we'll take the Beaujolais !"

BROUILLY

Appellation contrôlée

DOMAINE DE CONROY

Mme de Saint-Charles, propriétaire à Odenas (Rhône)   75 cl

SÉLECTIONNÉ ET MIS EN BOUTEILLE AU DOMAINE PAR
LES VINS GEORGES DUBŒUF, ROMANÈCHE-THORINS - 71

RÉCOLTE
1984

Beaujolais Nouveau

APPELLATION BEAUJOLAIS CONTRÔLÉE

ALC. 12.5 % VOL.   (Vm)   70 cl

Sélectionné et mis en bouteille par LES VINS MATHELIN à 69 Châtillon-d'Azergues France

N° 665   PRODUIT DE FRANCE

Pierres Dorées try to communicate when they entertain visitors who have fallen in love with their district and its wines. The *Gosiers Secs*, by contrast, are based at Haux-en-Beaujolais, acknowledged to be the original of Gabriel Chevallier's famous *Clochemerle*. Here the enthronements tend to be more robust, the initiate needs a strong constitution, a taste for risks, and a profound knowledge of the *Clochemerle* saga, born between a public urinal and a completely phony cure, in which the real Curé Ponosse is none other than the king of the Beaujolais chitterling, a certain Bobosse. But here, as elsewhere, the local wine is synonymous with revelry and good fellowship. Even the administration makes its contribution. I remember that during a recent meeting of the *Gosiers Secs*, the people who ran the Haut-Clochemerle Café had suffered a bereavement. There was no question of the tavern opening that day. But what would become of our party, if there was no place to go for a drink after the meeting? No problem: the Mayor ceded us the town hall for the evening, and there we continued to talk of Beaujolais after we had drunk it . . . The *Amis de Brouilly* are another typical Beaujolais association in the same world, though not exactly a brotherhood. Each year at the end of the summer when the harvest is about to begin, the Friends of Brouilly invite all lovers of Beaujolais to climb Mont Brouilly. When they reach the top of this local Ararat, they gather around the chapel of Notre-Dame du Raisin which has guarded the health of the grapes for over 130 years. Their rallying cry is a song:

> *Si le temps est beau,*
> *Il faut monter là-haut,*
> *Tu verras Montmerle . . .*

The only obligation to participants is that they must bring along their own food. Bread, wine and salt are served in unlimited quantities on tables round which people sit wherever they like, enjoying the glorious view of the Beaujolais and the Saône valley. As the hours go by, new friendships are made and the air is filled with good talk and good fellowship. Everyone here has already accepted the rule:

BROUILLY
PISSE VIEILLE
APPELLATION BROUILLY CONTROLÉE

Produit de France

Jean LATHUILIÈRE   75 cl
Viticulteur à CERCIÉ (Rhône)
MISE EN BOUTEILLES A LA PROPRIÉTÉ

DOMAINE DE LA TOUR DU BIEF

MOULIN-A-VENT

APPELLATION MOULIN-A-VENT CONTRÔLÉE

COMTE DE SPARRE, PROPRIÉTAIRE A CHÉNAS (RHONE) FRANCE

SÉLECTIONNÉ ET MIS EN BOUTEILLES AU DOMAINE PAR
LES VINS GEORGES DUBŒUF A 71720 ROMANÈCHE-THORINS   75 cl

LE BEAUJOL

J'aime beaucoup le mois de mai
Le mois d'aimer dans le muguet
Mais la saison que je préfère
C'est la saison des cimetières
Non pas pour déposer des fleurs
Sur ceux qui dorment dans mon cœur
Mais pour donner un coup d'palais
Dans le beaujolais.

C'est l'instant où Bacchus enfin
Nous donne son enfant divin
C'est l'heure où dans la chapelle
Autour des foudres de l'autel
La bande de cons bons enfants
Va taster religieusement
Le nouveau-né qu'on attendait
Notre beaujolais.

Malheur à l'intrus qui surgit
Au cours de la cérémonie
Au diable tous les faux goûteurs
Les m'as-tu-vu de connaisseurs
Ce n'est pas un cocktail mondain
Ni du folklore pour pantins
Mais une orgie de fins goulets
Au p'tit beaujolais.

C'est notre credo notre foi
Beaujol beaujol je crois en toi
C'est notre cri de ralliement
A beaujol on répond présent
C'est notre Pâque, notre Cène
C'est notre exorciseur de peine
Le magicien de nos pamphlets
Ce cher beaujolais.

O miracle et enchantement
La foi produit des faits troublants
Voilà que nous descend du ciel
Bacchus notre père éternel
Euterpe pendue à son bras
Fin saoule nous donne le La
Et c'est parti pour un couplet
Sacré beaujolais.

Si le monde tourne à l'envers
Depuis des décennies ma mère
C'est parce qu'à cette saison
Tout le paradis est fin rond
Il paraît que le vin d'ici
Éloigne l'eau de là et si
Vous prisez cet air guilleret
A moi vous ne devez rien mais
Tout au beaujolais.

Song written and put to music by Robert Grange

LE BEAUJOL

Paroles et Musique:
Robert GRANGE

C'est là que, posément, ils s'empliront la panse,
Que toujours soit honni celui qui mal y pense . . .

Later, as evening draws on, the wiser guests withdraw to the valley, but there always remains a die-hard lust of revellers, who decide to keep the evening going.

At dawn the next day, they will be seen emerging from some local cellar, still exchanging vows of eternal friendship. . . .

COME TO THE BEAUJOLAIS

The activities of the brotherhoods are supported and complemented by folk groups who perform only drinking songs, but also songs in praise of the countryside of the Beaujolais. Among these groups are: the *Cadets du Beaujolais* at Villefranche; the *Grappe Fleurie* at Fleurie; and the *Chansonnière du Beaujolais*, run by the composer Claude Morel at Châtillon-d'Azergues.

Other celebrants of the region are its poets, who have always been assiduous in its praises, and particularly in praise of its wine. Such as Emile de Villié:

Mon ami! Qui ne boit qu'un seul verre est boiteux:
Il n'a rien qu'une jambe! Il en faut au moins deux!
'Bis repetita placent' dit un juste adage!
Le premier verre est bon, l'autre l'est davantage!
Comme un magicien le noble vin s'avère.
Car fusses-tu plus laid qu'un singe ou qu'un corbeau,
Si tu pouvais te voir au travers de ton verre,
Tu te trouverais beau!

We would also cite the works of Francisque Norgelet, Pierre Aguétant and Léon Foillard, always remembering that Victor Hugo himself was moved to passion by the women gathering grapes in the Beaujolais. '. . . *ces cultivatrices penchées sur les vignes et dont on voyait surtout la première syllabe.*'

Come to the Beaujolais; you will find the descendants of Toine Dumontot awaiting you at their cellar doors, with the words:

SAINT-AMOUR
APPELLATION CONTROLÉE

RÉCOLTE 1980

CE VIN A OBTENU LE PRIX BACCHUS, RÉCOMPENSE ACCORDÉE AU MEILLEUR BEAUJOLAIS LORS DU CONCOURS DES VINS DE LA SAINT-VINCENT A MACON, LE 24 JANVIER 1981

SÉLECTIONNÉ ET MIS EN BOUTEILLES PAR
GEORGES DUBŒUF
ROMANÈCHE-THORINS, SAONE-ET-LOIRE, FRANCE
75 cl

177

BEAUJEU AND GNAFRON

The sole monument which indicates that Beaujeu is the historic capital of the Beaujolais is a statue in honour of Gnafron, one of the puppets of the Guignol Theatre at Lyon.

In the puppet show, Gnafron symbolizes the regrolleurs *(shoemakers or cobblers of the Quartier Saint-Georges in the old area of Lyon, which lay at the bottom of the hill of Fourrière). He carries a bottle of wine in one hand, being a great Beaujolais drinker. But nobody should call him a drunkard, which would be neither glorious nor edifying in someone who has been immortalized in stone.*

When the monument was unveiled on July 12, 1931, the very serious (but very witty) Senator for the Rhône, Justin Godart, defended Gnafron as follows:

'Gnafron is a wine lover. Offer him bad red wine, or a far fetched but fashionable cocktail, and he will turn away in sorrow. But if you give him the scent of a fine, fruity Beaujolais, or if the clear ruby light of one of our tender wines should catch his eye – his heart will swell for joy. And he will go in search of someone to share it with.
Gnafron must be properly understood.
Nobody should dare to call him a drunkard. That would be a slanderous falsehood.'

A drunkard is a miserable creature who doesn't know how to drink, who can drink anything, and who is thus not fit to do so. We should be sorry for poor devils like that – the only memorials they deserve are gravestones.

But Gnafron, when he drinks, pursues a healthy gaiety. Gnafron is unselfish. Before he brings his glass to his own lips, he passes it round the company in a spirit of fraternity.

Of course, sometimes he goes over the mark. But what is the mark? A line, drawn by somebody (God knows who) that must be reached but not overstepped. How convenient that one is allowed a happy mean. But where Beaujolais is concerned, it's a wise man indeed who knows first time (even second time) exactly where to stop. Try it you'll see. . . .

A Beaujolais house in the shadow of Château de Montmelas

BEAUJOLAIS
APPELLATION CONTRÔLÉE

PRODUIT DE FRANCE

1983 1983

BEAUJOLAIS-VILLAGES
PRIMEUR
APPELLATION BEAUJOLAIS-VILLAGES CONTRÔLÉE

700ml

Mis en bouteille par
Jacques DÉPAGNEUX à Villefranche (Rhône)

GEORGES. DUBŒUF

MOULIN-A-VENT
APPELLATION MOULIN-A-VENT CONTROLÉE

MIS EN BOUTEILLES PAR
LES VINS GEORGES DUBŒUF
71720 ROMANECHE - THORINS

75 cl

PRODUCED AND BOTTLED IN FRANCE

Il y a trois grands hommes sur la terre:
Napoléon pour la guerre,
Lamartine pour les ver,
Et Toine Dumontet
Pour le Beaujolais . . .

And if you hesitate to try *encore une tasse* after tasting two or three, one of the disciples of Pierre Collanges will inform you, in confidence, that 'the good Lord know me well. Last night, in a dream, he spoke to me, saying: "Pierre, drink deeply of it while you are still on earth, for I have nothing to match it in heaven . . ."'' Or perhaps your host will conjure you to finish the last glass with Catherine Bugnard's statement that 'It is better to stick one's nose into a glass of Beaujolais than into the affairs of others.'

And that is the way of the Beaujolais where hospitality is a religious rite, offered sincerely, as it was of old. It is the hospitality of two men who take stock of one another and who acknowledge their equality by the exchange of a simple toast. For although Beaujolais is the wine of happiness, it is also that of balance, moderation and serenity. As Emile de Villié has taught us:

Bois-en pour délecter ton âme et ton
*   palais*
Et chasser de ton sein toute humeur
*   importune*
Autant que pour narguer ou misère ou
*   fortune,*
Car sagesse est enclose au vin du
*   Beaujolais.*

Harvest's end at Chénas, 1926

Récolte 1981

Saint-Amour

Appellation Saint-Amour Contrôlée

75 cl

Mis en bouteille par : A. et R. Durand
Viticulteurs à Saint-Amour (Saône-et-Loire)

Pour Entrepôts Beaujolais - 71 - Chânes

DOMAINE DES JOURNETS
APPELLATION CHÉNAS CONTROLÉE

MIS EN BOUTEILLE PAR
THORIN VINS FINS S. A.

THORIN

71570 PONTANEVAUX
FRANCE

Juliénas

Domaine de Boischampt

APPELLATION JULIÉNAS CONTROLÉE

S. et G. DUPOND - PROPRIÉTAIRES à JULLIÉ (Rhône) - FRANCE

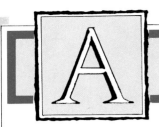

Félix BENOIT

In this uncertain modern world, which so often fills our bellies with bad food, we can do worse than look to the Beaujolais for inspiration. The cooking there is as honest as it is French, and the wines are not solemn old gentlemen who must be approached with appropriate ceremony. It is now many years since I tasted my first *saucisson en brioche* at Gabriel ('Gaby') Ferraton's establishment at Juliénas, the *Coq au Vin* . . . I remember that the meat had jealously preserved the juices and perfumes that are normally boiled away by the *court-bouillon*, and the wine went so well with it that I actually shed a tear of emotion.

This was the first tear of joy I had ever shed at the table. One remembers moments like that. Though time passes quietly, such things are not forgotten.

THE MÂCHON (MORNING MEAL) OF THE BEAUJOLAIS

If I may quote my old and sorely missed accomplice, Henry Clos Jouve:

'There are some lusciously presented dishes which completely fail to stimulate the appetite, just as there are very beautiful women who do not excite the least desire.'

Thank God, the Beaujolais never places its friends in such alarming predicaments; and as long as it relies

Advertisement for the famous cooking school, Tsuji (*Osaka*), located in the Beaujolais region at the Chateau de l'Eclair.

on the *Mâchon* as the blueprint for a meal, the word fraternity will retain its meaning. Justin Godart, unconditional lover of the Beaujolais who was so nearly elected President of the Republic, was one day heard to proclaim (fork in hand) that: '. . . There are those who eat truffles and drink champagne all day, but that's nothing beside a good *mâchon*.' Let us emphasize, then, that the *mâchon* remains the most convincing evidence of the profound affinities between the best elements of the Lyonnais and the Beaujolais.

When one is partaking of a *mâchon*, '*le café-crème commence au jambonneau*', as everyone knows. Marcel Grancher

used to have this dictum on display in his cellars. After the war, Grancher founded his *Franc Mâchonnerie*, in company with a few friends. This became an elite of 'morning eaters', with a Paris contingent that remained loyal to the Beaujolais origins. Let us not forget, either, that the marionnette cobbler Gnafron owed his legendary humour and deep manly voice to his ample consumption of Beaujolais. A memorial to him has been raised at Beaujeu, and I always doff my hat to it when I pass. Gnafron knew that the *mâchon* is a kind of call to mass, which can occur at any hour of the day; and as a true believer, he would never miss a single communion.

This happy man could not read, but if he had survived to discover the shores of culture, he would undoubtedly have approved of this exhortation by the Lyonnais writer Marinus Memillon:

'Drink, my friends, and drink new Beaujolais if you can. It is a wine which fills the brains with the tightest of froths. One can drink it in great quantity. And it would bring a smile to the lips of M Paul Valéry himself.'

FOOD OF THE BEAUJOLAIS IN FORMER TIMES

The lasting values of traditional Beaujolais cuisine are intermingled with those of Lyonnais cooking, which in turn has learned much from its neighbours of Bresse and Bugey. Thus to speak of interdependency among these traditions is perfectly legitimate.

'Beaujolais' is the magic word that illuminates all. That unforgettable writer Francis Ammategui tells us how, in his book *Le Plaisir des Mets*: 'The force of expansion contained in these ten simple letters is equivalent to the power that split the atom. What, in fact, are the salient dates in the history of the world? 1453: the capture of Constantinople by the

Turks. 1789: the capture of the Bastille by the people of Paris. 1945: the capture of France by the Beaujolais.'

The dishes listed below are some of those which were eaten regularly by families in the Beaujolais, well before 1945; though some of them have fallen out of favour in our own time, they may well recover their former popularity. At least, I hope so.

Cooking with wine cuttings is now relatively rare. The dry twigs are ideal for grills and sautés.

Soupe au vin is a dish that has almost disappeared. The old wine-growers have gone the way of their fathers, and very few people still pour a glass of Beaujolais into their *Bouillon gras* at meals. This old recipe could be refined in the following way: peel, clean and dice one carrot, one leek (the white part), a turnip and an onion. Blanch these vegetables with one soupspoonful of butter. Add half a bottle of Beaujolais (preferably Morgon or Fleurie) and reduce on a low fire till thick. Then add beef or chicken bouillon, and simmer for one hour; finally, scatter two soupspoonfuls of tapioca and allow to cook for twenty minutes longer.

Tartines au vin used to be a customary snack between meals for children and grandparents. They are very simple and taste very good. Cut slices of country bread and toast on both sides. Wet them quickly in water and place them on very hot plates. Then pour Beaujolais over them and powder liberally with sugar.

Ragoût de Mouton au Beaujolais is a great speciality of the region, which, though less delicate than *coq au vin*, is nonetheless much prized by lovers of the local cooking. Here is the recipe: take two or three pounds of breast or shoulder of lamb and cut into small pieces. Add salt, pepper and nutmeg. Melt two spoonfuls of lard in a big frying pan, along with a hundred grams of lean bacon. To this add the pieces of lamb, stirring well till brown; then add flour and a large bowl of hot bouillon, with two glasses of hot Beaujolais (preferably old). To this mixture add garlic, thyme, parsley, bayleaf, small potatoes (peeled) and enough hot water to

THE GOOD FARE OF VILLEFRANCHE

At Villefranche, people in the know are thronging to Le Restaurant de la Benoîte. We in Paris have no equivalent for this place, and the kitchen is still ruled by a lady cook who is still in full possession of her marvellous gifts. Everywhere there are jugs of Beaujolais – and what Beaujolais – to assuage the thirst and awaken the tastebuds, marking each stage of an innocent but very powerful pleasure.

It is strange to think that so many people, rich but ill-informed, who see the outer shells of things rather than their reality, can go to those abominable espagnoles, *or those palaces of soft, limp, tasteless meat; in a word, to eat the muck now known as 'European', which gives one stomach-ache and is served by ceremonious waiters; when, just round the corner, they could dine far more cheaply on the best and rarest dishes of the world's finest traditional cookery. But, things are perfectly all right as they are; it would be regrettable if these gilded bounders thrown up by our troubled times should ever know the mental delights that can come from honest wine, bread made from pure flour, and a white local cheese.*

Everyone knows that Beaujolais is an incomparable table wine. It is cool, delicate without weakness, fruity, exquisite to drink and drink again; and it does not overwhelm the taste of white meat. It stresses, as none other can, the buttery thickened sauces which are the glory of Lyonnais cooking and which are never so perfect anywhere else. Beaujolais leaves no headaches, bladder aches, or belly aches. It is reliable and healthy par excellence; *and every doctor treating patients for dyspepsia should send them to Lyon or the Beaujolais, with the recommendation that they take a cure of good food, washed down with Fleurie or Morgon.*

Léon Daudet, from the *Almanach du Beaujolais*, 1956

Edouard Herriot and his friends

MENU
DU 14 SEPTEMBRE 1897

Potage Saint-Germain
Hors d'Œuvre variés
Melon Sibérienne
Filet de Bœuf Madère
Timbale Parisienne
Canetons de Rouen à la Périgueux
Truite saumonée Sauce verte
Petits Pois à la Paysanne
Cuissot de Chevreuil Grand-Veneur
Salade de Saison
Jambon d'York à la Gelée
Ecrevisses en Belle-Vue
Parfait Glacé
Gaufrettes
Pièce Montée
Gâteau Historique
Fruits
Desserts Assortis

VINS
Vigneul 1887
Moulin-à-Vent
Volnay
Mercurey
Saint-Emilion
Champagne Frappé

RENÉ WIENER, NANCY.

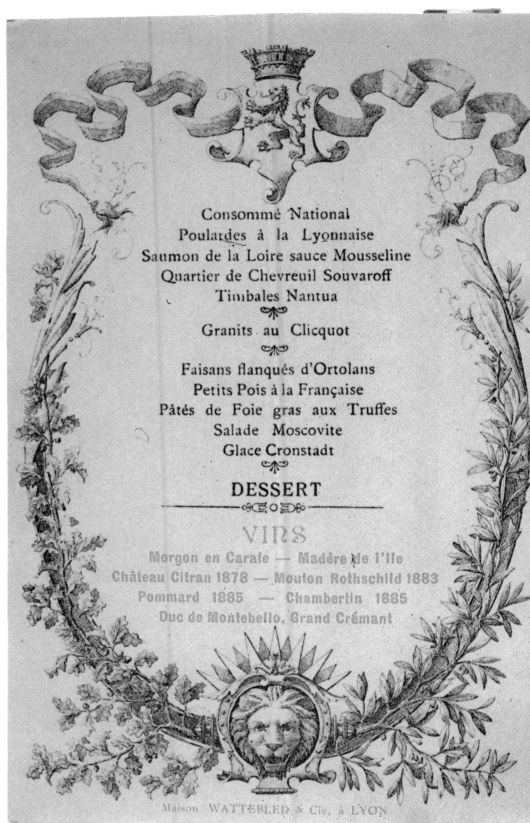

Consommé National
Poulardes à la Lyonnaise
Saumon de la Loire sauce Mousseline
Quartier de Chevreuil Souvaroff
Timbales Nantua

Granits au Clicquot

Faisans flanqués d'Ortolans
Petits Pois à la Française
Pâtés de Foie gras aux Truffes
Salade Moscovite
Glace Cronstadt

DESSERT

VINS
Morgon en Carafe — Madère de l'Ile
Château Citran 1878 — Mouton Rothschild 1883
Pommard 1885 — Chambertin 1885
Duc de Montebello, Grand Crémant

Maison WATTEBLED & Cie, à LYON

MENU EN L'HONNEUR DE L'ESCADRE RUSSE, AU TEMPS DES TSARS (COLLECTION PARTICULIÈRE).

Національный консоммé

Ліонскія пулярды

Семьга изъ Люары съ кисейнымъ соусомъ

Козуля по Суворовски

Нантуйскія тимбали

◦──◦─◦

Кликотовскіе граниты

◦──◦─◦

Фазаны съ овсянкой

Горошокъ по-французски

Пирогъ изъ гусиной печени съ труфлями

Московскій салад

Кронштадтское мороженое

Дессеръ

ВИНА

Моргонъ въ графинахъ—Мадера съ острова
Шато Ситранъ 1878 — Мутонъ Ротшильдъ
Помаръ 1885 — Шамбертенъ 1885
Дюкъ Монтебелло, Гранъ Кремант

Ліонъ, Типографія А. Шторка

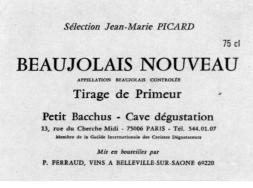

cover. Bring to the boil, then pour into a large casserole, cover and cook till done.

Chamour derives from a word in the local dialect meaning a sort of solid pumpkin flan. This was formerly a dish offered to the grape harvesters in generous measure, so generous that these seasonal workers came to be known as *Chamouris*. *Chamour* was made in the Biblical fashion: boil pieces of a large pumpkin till fairly soft; when done, remove from the water and dry carefully. Then mash with a fork, mixing in two or three piled tablespoonfuls of crushed biscuits. Sugar and salt lightly, and add a generous handful of white flour and two or three beaten eggs. Mix well and place in a large earthenware pan which can go in the oven without cracking. Scatter breadcrumbs over the top, with plenty of butter, then cook in a medium oven until a knife can be pushed into the *Chamour* and come out clean.

Pognou is a delicacy made with bread dough, mixed up with plenty of butter and a little sugar, to which are added (according to the season) cherries and slices of apple or pear. This, when baked, produces a heavy cake, excellent served with a very cool Beaujolais.

Saucisson au Vin was not made with ordinary sausage, but with the country version, cut thick and cooked in a stewpot in pure Beaujolais. To this was added coarse ground pepper, a bunch of thyme and some cinnamon.

This simple cuisine is what people ate at home. It never reached the restaurants, and it dates from the time of those memorable end-of-harvest or end-of-pressing banquets. The wine-growers' wives used to excel themselves at these glorious feasts: *Saucisson au vin*, *Boeuf bouilli*, *Chapon au bouillon gras* (Capon) served with a huge platter of rice . . . and *Chamour* as a side-dish, vegetable or dessert. As a digestive, a liqueur wine known as *L'Ami de l'Homme* would be served; this was a kind of Beaujolais elixir, composed of sweet white wine from the press to which one glassful per litre of old *marc* was added (not to be confused with the deadly *rikiki*).

Well may we thank our Lady of Brouilly for all these good things. Thanks to her intervention, miracles can still happen.

Recent initiatives have shown that nothing can restrain gastronomic research from continuing its progress. For example, only recently, M Gérard Chaut, of Chamelet, is said to have invented a new kind of *grappille*, based on a mixture of nuts, honey and marc.

LES COCHONNAILLES DU PAYS

Any *saucisson* worthy of the name is conscientiously and affectionately made. They are eaten at christenings, weddings and funerals . . . and many people consume them in the early morning for breakfast. In the Beaujolais, much fuss is made over the *rosette* of sausage, which is taken with the wine of the same year. The *rosette* is a high quality sausage, proud of being embossed in the rectum of the pig – hence its name, because a pig's anus has a certain resemblance to a rose, and even to a certain French official decoration.

The Jemo sausage, to take an example, arrives swaddled in a kind of net; the meat is contained in a part of the pig's intestine, and while drying takes the plump shape of a doll – hence its name.

Among the hot sausages, nothing could be better than *Andouillettes Tirées à la Ficelle*, as they are prepared in the marvellous charcuteries along the Calade. These *andouillettes* have made the reputation of the exquisite René Besson, known as 'Bobosse', an important regional figure who has lately acquired an international standing from his base at Saint-Jean-D'Ardières. His *andouillettes* are based on the calf's crow, and never cause any trouble to people with delicate stomachs. A course of grilled *andouillettes* is even cited as a cure for dyspepsia.

All that remains to describe is the oily *Sabodet*, with its distant Dauphinois origins. This is a pot-bellied sausage, stuffed with pork rind and jowls. It is eaten well cooked, still wet from the hot bouillon, and it is

BALLADE DES FROMAGES DE CHÈVRES

Doux comme un miel de l'Hélicon,
Les fromages de la fermière,
Vont, bien rangés dans leur panière,
Au marché de Villié-Morgon.
Las ! Ils ont quitté leur chaumière
Aussi restent-ils tout pâlots
D'avoir laissé les sapinières
De Marchampt ou des Écharmeaux.

Ce sont les petits chevrotons
Plus fins que le plus fin gruyère,
Ressource de la cuisinière
Après le gigot de mouton.
Parfois durs comme de la pierre
Ou tendres comme du gâteau,
On croit respirer la bruyère
De Marchampt ou des Écharmeaux.

Fernand Velon: extract from Le pays et le Vin
Beaujolais *by Léon Foillard and Tony David,*
1929

189

served on a bed of lentils. All these *cochonnailles* have inspired the poets of the Beaujolais and given good reasons for returning there to many a trencherman. The brilliant Colette, remembering an evening spent at Brouilly with Claude Geoffray, the lord of Château-Thivin, wrote: '. . . our meal was a homage to hams well wrapped in fat, sausages like new leather, and a certain cheese, referred to as *fort*, which provokes an unslakeable thirst.'

THE CANARD ENCHAÎNÉ AT JULIÉNAS

The fame of Juliénas in the columns of the mischievous *Canard Enchaîné* dates from the 1930s. It is still heavily featured and this admirable publication acts as a Beaujolais bridgehead to Paris. The link derives from an enthusiastic friendship between Toto Dubois and Victor Peyret, both of whom are now dead. Before devoting himself to the vines of Juliénas, Toto Dubois was a journalist at the Lyon Salut Public. He had fought in the First World War, during which he had come to know Maurice Maréchal, the future head of the *Canard Enchaîné*. (The *Canard* started out as a simple gazette distributed in the trenches.) Maréchal, hearing that his friend was living at Juliénas, came to see him, and subsequently brought along his most talented journalists: those who liked good wine. Toto Dubois offered so generous a welcome that the *Canard*'s pilgrimage became a regular occurrence. Henri Quilas designed the menu for the Coq au Vin restaurant, and during one famous lunch there on September 29, 1934, the entire editorial staff of the *Canard* was present: Maréchal, Tréno, Pol Ferjac, Pierre Bénard, Pruvost, Pédro, Quilac, Pavil and many more.

Victor Peyret was Toto Dubois' successor; he was a grower at the Château des Capitans at Juliénas. Peyret was also a great lover of arts and letters, and the founder of the Cellier de la Vieille Eglise. He never missed a chance to join the feasts arranged for the *Canard*, nor to visit their offices when he passed through

Paris. His contribution to Juliénas has been recognized in our own time by the 1965 attribution of a Victor Peyret Prize, which is given every year in mid-November, at the Fête des Vins. Naturally, associates of the *Canard Enchaîné* have often been among the prizewinners.

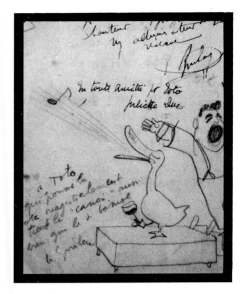

The back of the famous 1934 menu at the Coq au Vin, inscribed by the journalists of the Canard Enchaîné

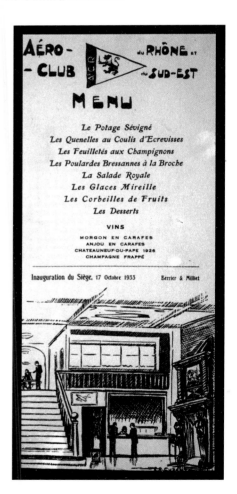

ACKNOWLEDGEMENTS

The authors and publishers would like to thank the following for supplying material:

Mme DARGENT,

Mme DEVELAY,

P. AUDRAS,

H. BESSON,

BRAULT,

G. CANARD,

G. CLAUDEY,

G. COMPARAT,

J.-L. DESVIGNES,

G. DUBŒUF,

P. FAURE,

J. FEU,

PH. FOURNEAU,

A. GOUGENHEIM,

CH. MÉRIEUX,

P. MARINGUE,

ORSI,

M. PASQUIER-DESVIGNES

P. PERICHON-MESLAY,

F. ROSTAING,

P. SARRAU,

J. TIXIER,

J.-P. THORIN,

L'Union interprofessionnelle
des vins du Beaujolais,

Le Centre d'Arts et Traditions Populaires
de Villefranche-sur-Saône